OVERSEERS OF THE POOR

Frank —
Thanks for all
the help.

THE CHICAGO SERIES IN LAW AND SOCIETY
Edited by William M. O'Barr and John M. Conley

OVERSEERS OF THE POOR

SURVEILLANCE, RESISTANCE, AND

THE LIMITS OF PRIVACY

John Gilliom

THE UNIVERSITY OF CHICAGO PRESS

CHICAGO AND LONDON

JOHN GILLIOM is associate professor of political science at Ohio University. He is the author of *Surveillance, Privacy, and the Law: Employee Drug Testing and the Politics of Social Control.*

The University of Chicago Press, Chicago 60637
The University of Chicago Press, Ltd., London
© 2001 by The University of Chicago
All rights reserved. Published 2001
Printed in the United States of America

10 09 08 07 06 05 04 03 02 01   5 4 3 2 1

ISBN (cloth): 0-226-29360-2
ISBN (paper): 0-226-29361-0

Portions of chapters 3 and 4 are adapted from John Gilliom, "Everyday Surveillance, Everyday Resistance: Computer Monitoring in the Lives of the Appalachian Poor," *Studies in Law, Politics, and Society* 16 (1997): 275–92, with the permission of Elsevier Science.

Library of Congress Cataloging-in-Publication

Gilliom, John, 1960–
    Overseers of the poor : surveillance, resistance, and the limits of privacy / John Gilliom.
        p.   cm. — (The Chicago series in law and society)
    Includes bibliographical references and index.
    ISBN 0-226-29360-2 (cloth) — ISBN 0-226-29361-0 (pbk.)
    1. Public welfare—Law and legislation—United States.
2. Government information—United States. 3. Electronic surveillance—United States. 4. Privacy, Right of—United States. 5. Welfare recipients—Civil rights—United States.
I. Title. II. Series.
    KF3720 .G55   2001
    342.73'0858—dc21   2001002841

For my parents

In colonial times, communities often named a public official to monitor the indigent and provide for their relief or eviction.
This official was
The Overseer of the Poor.

CONTENTS

ONE DAY IN THE LATE SUMMER of 1999, a police helicopter found a large garden of marijuana growing in the federal forest about a third of a mile from my family's home. That evening, the local sheriff's department obtained a warrant and searched our house from top to bottom. Later, as I helped my five-year-old daughter clean up her room and tried to explain why "Officer Friendly" had trashed it, my thoughts swirled in anger. The violence that had been done to my children's world, the fear that I felt about potential prosecution or the civil forfeiture of our home, the personal rage I felt toward the men who had done this—these currents and others overwhelmed my consciousness as I worked through the events that are recounted in the epilogue to this book. Through it all, I became even more convinced about an idea that I have been exploring for the last few years: that our culture made a bad bet when it turned to something called "the right to privacy" as the catchall concept for describing, evaluating, and challenging invasions like this. It was a bad bet not only because the right to privacy so obviously fails to protect us from increasing invasions, but also because it fails to come even close to accounting for the powerful combination of anger, powerlessness, domination, and fear that my family experienced. The aging legal concept was simply failing to help us make sense of and act upon our world.

A year later, in the summer of 2000, I encountered another episode in the story of surveillance, but this time I had more company. It was around then that Americans heard about the latest in an ongoing series of powerful new tools with which authorities can watch what we do. This was "Carnivore," the FBI's aptly named Internet surveillance system. There was a flurry of political controversy when it was learned that Carnivore gave federal authorities the unprecedented capacity to locate and capture specific e-mail and other traffic going through the computers of Internet Service Providers. Listening to the news on National Public Radio, I heard the story about Carnivore conclude with these words: *"Privacy advocates argue that the new technology poses a threat to privacy rights."*

Despite the burst of attention, Carnivore was, in a way, nothing new. Surveillance measures that previous generations would have described as Orwellian now strike contemporary Americans as routine business. Global positioning satellites; trackable cars and cell phones; closed-circuit television cameras in parks and streets; computer data matching of banking, insurance, and taxation records; "cookies" and other ways of monitoring Internet activity; the drug testing of students, workers, and welfare clients: all are now more or less routine parts of American life. And NPR's tag line was certainly nothing new. It could have wrapped up almost any news report about these recent advancements in the state's capacity to see and know. In all of these cases our public discourse consistently inserts the prefabricated, repetitive, uninformative, lawsome, and dreadfully obvious line: *"Privacy advocates argue that the new technology poses a threat to privacy rights."*

This book grew out of a sense that our public conversation about surveillance policy and technology was sadly deficient and that better ways of talking about surveillance were already out there in the lives and minds of Americans who were experiencing these transformations; that behind, below, betwixt, or beside the public discourse of privacy rights were other ways of speaking and thinking about surveillance that could and should inform our confrontation with these issues. Therefore, in this work, you will find no excursions to visit aging legal texts or the writings of dead philosophers, few official policy experts or authorities, and almost no attorneys, judges or privacy advocates. What you will find is people who are seldom seen and rarely heard, but who may well know more about the nature and implications of surveillance than all of the foregoing experts put together—low-income American mothers who live every day with the advanced surveillance capacity of the modern welfare state. In their pursuit of food, health care, and shelter for their families, they are watched, analyzed, assessed, monitored, checked, and reevaluated in an ongoing process involving supercomputers, caseworkers, fraud control agents, grocers, and neighbors. They *know* surveillance. From the words of these women, who are far removed from the official discussions by differences in experience, class, gender, identity, and political status, we can learn about both the limits and failures of our conventional ways of speaking and the potential terms and concerns of a new agenda. And we can also learn something, I hope, about the women themselves and how they live their often sad, sometimes frightening, and frequently quite noble lives attempting to mother below the poverty line in rural Appalachia.

Because this book touches on many themes—surveillance, privacy rights, welfare policy, poverty, gender—readers are likely to come to it for different reasons. Some will approach this book as a story about law: about rights, about rules, about enforcement and evasion. Many will see it as a book about new technologies of surveillance and the decreasing spaces for privacy in our information-driven society. Others will approach it as a story about the poor, their domination, and ways in which they struggle. Still others will see it as a story about women, their subjugation, and the vitality and powers with which they approach the world. For still others, this may be a book about welfare administration, "fraud control," computerization, Appalachian life, or the languages of politics. All of these readings are welcomed, although I am sure that, as a specialized take on any of these particular interests, this book has left much unsaid.

For me, this has become a book about human struggle over ways of seeing and knowing. Surveillance programs are ways of seeing and knowing the world. They assert values, identify priorities, define possibilities, and police the departures. In so doing, they build important structures of meaning that help to shape our world and our place within it. Subjects of surveillance frequently challenge and resist these acts of observation, depiction, and control, and these struggles between the watchers and the watched mark important political battles. And just as a surveillance system is just one among many ways of seeing the world, there are many ways to "see" surveillance—state bureaucrats, police officers, civil liberties attorneys, law professors, journalists, and the subjects of surveillance all see and know a surveillance system in different ways. This work is committed to advancing the views of those who have been silenced for so long. Not just because they deserve to be heard but because of what their account can teach about the new forms of power that we all confront.

•

It is impossible to picture and recognize all of the people who contributed to this project. Many—the dozens of anonymous women in rural southeastern Ohio who consented to talk with us—I have heard only on tape. My profound thanks to all of these people for sharing their understandings, stories, and wisdom. Cindy Baker and Karen Mallon were outstanding and patient teachers, researchers, and interviewers who were essential to the success of the fieldwork; when the term "we" is used in this book's discussions of interviews and interview results, it is to these remarkable teammates that I refer. Jack Frech, Bob Gallagher, and many other administrators, caseworkers, auditors, fraud control agents, and computer consultants deserve my thanks for helping me to understand the world of human services information and administration. George Bain led me to the rich archives of the home visit records of the early Mother's Pension programs in our region. My beloved uncle, Steve Gorbics, generously shared the stories of his Depression-era childhood. Thanks also go out to the Ohio University Research Committee for support in beginning this project, to my colleagues in the Department of Political Science at Ohio University for creating such an ideal workplace, and to the Law and Society Association for all the good things that it does.

As the manuscript began to take form, my debts expanded. Susan Burgess, John Conley, Chuck Epp, Guy Goodwin, Amy King, Kate Leeman, Michael McCann, Neal Milner, Austin Sarat, Stuart Scheingold, Helena Silverstein, Taka Suzuki, and John Tryneski were all kind enough to read and share their perceptions on earlier drafts. If I had followed all of their advice, this would be a much better (and longer) book. Thanks also to Don Adleta, who shared his infinite talent in designing the cover. My thanks as well to the many others who shared their insights regarding various aspects of the project: Sara Cobb, David Engel, Jon Goldberg-Hiller, Joel Handler, and Frank

Munger. Julie White is an outstanding friend and colleague who not only read the manuscript, but shared her understandings, wisdom, and books throughout this process.

Finally, I want to thank my family—Amy, Alden, and Ryan—a family that soars beyond any dream of what could be.

You have to watch every step like you are in prison. All the time you are on welfare, yeah, you are in prison. Someone is watching like a guard. Someone is watching over you and you are hoping every day that you won't go up the creek, so to speak, and (that you will) get out alive in any way, shape, or form. You know, "Did I remember to say that a child moved in?" "Did I remember to say that a child moved out?" And, "Did I call within that five days?" You know . . . making sure all the time. . . . It's as close to a prison that I can think of.

Mary, a forty-something mother of three, on welfare,
in Appalachian Ohio

Mary is describing her condition of comprehensive surveillance and regulation. There are many who watch her: welfare caseworkers and other bureaucrats, neighbors and community members, and most recently, something known as CRIS-E—the Client Registry Information System–Enhanced. CRIS-E is a computer system that manages welfare cases, implements regular number matches and verification programs, and issues automatic warnings and compliance demands for all of the state's welfare clients. For Mary, and many others, this system of welfare surveillance instills an ongoing awareness of a power that can catch them in a little slip or some petty fraud and punish them with financial penalties, the loss of health care and food stamps, or a prison more literal than the one of which Mary speaks.

This book is about surveillance and about how people like Mary cope with its ongoing presence in their daily lives. *Surveillance*, as used here, refers not to the cloak-and-dagger stuff of hidden microphones, but to the increasingly routine use of personal data and systematic information in the administration of institutions, agencies, and businesses. Over the past few decades, there have been dramatic expansions in the quality, the breadth, and the intensity of programs that use new generations of technology for gathering, storing, sharing, and using information. Indeed, if we add up the frequently overlapping profiles encompassing medical records, academic and professional performance, credit ratings, consumer behavior, insurance records, driving records, law enforcement data, welfare agency information, child support enforcement programs, Internet communications, and other information systems, it is safe to say that much of the significant activity of our lives is now subject to systematic observation and analysis. And as these systems are enhanced with rapidly emerging new technologies for computerized analysis and exchange, biological assessment and identification, and increasingly automated monitoring of communications, financial conduct, and travel, it seems clear that we are truly entering a "new landscape" of surveillance and regulation (Bennett and Grant 1999; Agre and Rotenberg 1997; Regan 1995; Gandy 1993; Dandeker 1990; Marx 1986).

If this is the "Information Age," it should hardly be surprising that information gathering and management have moved to the center of governance. By now, virtually any public or private agency handling large numbers of people is likely to have an advanced surveillance capacity as a central part of its daily operations. On the basis of these systems of information, decisions are made regarding the lives and life prospects of everyone from suspected criminals to prospective home buyers, and from students to welfare families. People have always been observed and evaluated by kin, by neighbors, by employers, and by strangers, but now both watching and being watched have become more complex, more systematic, and in some areas, far more critical in the everyday lives of families and individuals. In a way, then, we are all becoming more like Mary. Because of this, a new politics has been created, or, rather, an old politics has changed and become more important and pervasive—the politics of surveillance.

The politics of surveillance necessarily include the dynamics of power and domination. The very idea of "surveillance"—roughly translated as *watching from above*—implies that the observer is in a position of dominance over the observed. Related terms like *supervisor*, or the one chosen for the title of this work, *overseer*, remind us that surveillance is not a mere glance exchanged between equals—it is both an expression and instrument of power. Surveillance of human behavior is in place to control human behavior, whether by limiting access to programs or institutions, monitoring and affecting behavior within those arenas, or otherwise enforcing rules and norms by observing and recording acts of compliance and deviance. It is hard to imagine a surveillance and control program being applied in a context that lacked regular efforts or tendencies to violate rules or norms; therefore struggles over power, information, exposure, and secrecy are virtually guaranteed to be part of the politics of surveillance. Mary, for example, rented a room to a friend but hid the small extra income from the welfare office. Businesses, as well as middle- and upper-class families, engage in the national sport of avoiding taxation by mastering the terms of the surveillance and collection system and playing them to their best advantage. Fast drivers use radar detection to avoid speeding tickets. Unlucky drivers seek to cover minor accidents with cash to avoid alerting the advanced surveillance systems of insurance companies. Savvy users of the Internet encrypt or anonymize their browsing and communication. College students traffic in false identification to beat the age limits on the consumption of alcohol. As public and private authorities seek to detect and control a wider variety of behavior using programs of intensive surveillance, millions of people become a little bit more like Mary; surrounded by checkpoints that are often unseen and working the system the best that we can.

As a political scientist—one who studies governance, politics, and power—I undertook this project in the hope of contributing to our understandings about, first, what goes on in the politics of surveillance; second, what effects sustained surveillance has on people's lives; and, third, what it is that people say and do as they struggle with new policies of surveillance. Although the topics of surveillance, policy, and privacy are the subjects of dozens of books, we still know relatively little about the everyday politics of surveillance as they are experienced and explained by those who are among the most closely watched. After working with the existing scholarly literature on surveillance and privacy, I felt that much of it, with noteworthy exceptions, was simply overrun with the agendas and vocabularies of lawyers, academics, and policymakers. It was *their* language, *their* concerns, and *their* agendas that appeared to be the dominant interest in most public discourse on the topic (see also, Davies 1999).[1]

So, while we have heard much about long-standing debates over the legal concepts of "privacy" and "due process" and about policymaking concerns like effectiveness, impact, and risk, we have heard relatively little about the everyday American conversations and struggles over the actual implementation of surveillance policies. Frequent opinion surveys have asked the public to agree or disagree with precoded questions about these topics—and they are persistently concerned about their "privacy" (Davies 1999; Regan 1995)—but surveys can rarely go beyond the simplest terms of the established vocabulary. This project seeks to learn what's going on out there away from the opinion polls, policy analyses, and legal briefs. Is this thing called "privacy" really the crux of concern for a subject of surveillance? Is the legalistic framework of "rights," of "the right to due process" and the "right to privacy," a helpful and productive way to speak about people's concerns in this area? And are the recognized arenas of legislatures, courts, and public debate the places where the struggles over surveillance will be played out? Can new languages and perspectives enhance our struggles to manage and understand the new alignments of power manifest in the surveillance revolution?

These are big questions and this book only begins a process of trying to answer them. To make that beginning, I wanted to find a way to bring the voices and experiences of the surveilled into our struggles to understand what surveillance is and into the public discussions about the ongoing revolution in surveillance technology and policy. I wanted to learn how they perceived the system of surveillance, how they spoke of it, and how they coped with it in their daily lives. Therefore, in the mid-1990s, I began a research project centering on how a group of welfare mothers in Appalachian Ohio experienced the impact of a major new computerized surveillance and information system in welfare administration.[2] The surveillance system they live with, explained in chapter 1, gives welfare and law enforcement authorities the power to make regular data sweeps which can detect virtually any recorded income or investment-returns that an individual may receive. It also automates the case monitoring and review process that is a regular part of receiving welfare and shifts the previously unwieldy county-by-county record-keeping system into one unified matrix. With this sophisticated new "Client Information System," administrators were able to organize, enhance, and expand the various dimensions of scrutiny that have long been part of American welfare. The system was, I will argue, the new "overseer of the poor." In a computerized aspirant to the "panopticon"—Jeremy Bentham's name for an ideal prison in which everyone is watched, all the time—the state's power tries to be a constant presence in the lives of the poor.

To learn about the nature and impact of these innovations, we spoke with roughly fifty welfare mothers. Under the cloak of anonymity, they joined in taped conversations touching upon the stories of their lives, their experiences on welfare, and their experiences with and reactions to the new surveillance program. Because of our hope to have these conversations take place in a climate of trust and familiarity, the semistructured interviews were arranged and conducted by two women who were themselves recent AFDC (Aid to Families with Dependent Children) clients from the local area. Moreover, because we hoped that the interviews would convey the women's vernacular terms and informal thoughts on these topics, we were very careful to avoid the official vocabulary of surveillance and privacy and to embed our conversations about surveillance in a context of everyday life and casual talk. (The research methods are discussed in chapter 2.)

The stories that we heard were diverse and multifaceted, but amid that diversity an important theme began to emerge. Although they live in a culture that is said to be overrun with rights claims and among the most litigious and law-oriented on earth (see, for example, Glendon 1991), and although they were talking about a policy area that has been almost totally defined by debates over legal rights to privacy and due process, the women who are at the center of this book said very little about the idea of rights, or of privacy, or of other potentially protective or emancipatory legal claims.[3] What emerged from these conversations was, in fact, a widely shared and principled critique of surveillance, but one that had very little to do with the ongoing main-stream legal and policy debates about rights to privacy and due process. Instead, the mothers complained about the hassle and degradation caused by surveillance and the ways that it hindered their ability to meet the needs of their families. They advanced few claims tied to the right of privacy; instead, they told particular stories about daily need and about the power of surveillance to both make their needs greater and limit their capacity to meet them. They made references not to the great claim of due process, but to their own struggles to cope and to the power of surveillance to thwart them. In their need and anger, they mounted no litigation or protest campaigns, but engaged in necessarily quiet practices of everyday resistance and evasion to beat, as best they could, the powers of surveillance.

In many ways, then, these women eschew the prevailing languages and tactics of the privacy-rights paradigm to position their critique of surveillance within a framework emphasizing their needs, their practical problems, and their duty to care for their children.[4] In so doing, they build a critique of surveillance that is based in the realities and demands of everyday life. They also appear to give voice to what has been called the "ethic of care," a political language that centers on needs, relationships, and interdependency and may, therefore, be distinct from the more conventional liberal thinking and its emphasis on abstract principles and individualistic rights claims.[5] In resonance with the types of claims-making found among other oppressed groups and with a long-standing though often subjugated "maternalist" ideology in American welfare (Bussiere 1997; Gordon 1994), our conversations returned again and again to what was clearly, for these women, the "business at hand"—getting their families through another day.

In their struggles to get through the day, the women we talked with also engage in a widespread and little-noticed form of antisurveillance "politics"—they do things that politicians and many (but not all) welfare officials might view as fraud, evasion, or cheating, but that the welfare mothers see as some of their only options for struggling with the powers of the state. As they hide little bits of extra money, or sneak an extra boarder or family member into their home, they make no grand challenges to an invasive bureaucracy, but they do enhance their material lives and create small and necessary spaces of personal control and autonomy. And since the system of welfare surveillance is specifically designed to prevent these forbidden material improvements and to eliminate personal control and autonomy, we can only see the work of these welfare mothers as an apparently significant and widespread form of antisurveillance politics.

These findings help cast important light on the long-standing debates about surveillance and privacy. From as far back as the famous 1890 *Harvard Law Review* article on "The Right to Privacy" by Warren and Brandeis, to Alan Westin's important and influential 1967 work *Privacy and Freedom*, to more recent court opinions and academic works on these topics (see Gellman 1997; Regan 1995), the idea of "a right to privacy" has been the pivotal concept in our efforts to understand, discuss, and combat the increasing use of surveillance policies. It has, as such, shaped our very understandings of surveillance itself, leaving us almost voiceless if we are asked to speak or think about the problem of surveillance without turning to the idea of privacy.

Rogers Smith (1988) has argued that rhetorical practices can become so fixed and influential that they come to act as "institutions"—shaping our capacity for conversation, action, and politics. To my eye, the "privacy paradigm" which has dominated and framed our comprehension and discussion of surveillance for well over a century is just such an institution. And it is an institution in trouble. On the policy front, hardly anyone is willing to conclude that the current approach to privacy and surveillance is producing many effective limits on the expansion of surveillance; indeed, a long list of works researching the effectiveness of privacy law in limiting the expansion of new surveillance technologies suggests that, with the exception of some sporadic applications of procedural guarantees, there is little for privacy advocates to celebrate (Gellman 1997; Regan 1995; Gilliom 1994; Flaherty 1989). Politically, the privacy paradigm is pitted against important social values like safety, crime-fighting, and national security. In these contests it has failed to sufficiently galvanize publics or legislatures into producing legislation with the capacity to effectively control surveillance (Regan 1995).[6] Legally, conservative judicial decisions of recent decades have reduced the idea of a right to privacy to a flexible and lesser factor in their decisions largely approving new forms of searching and watching (Gilliom 1994; Gellman 1997). Conceptually, the privacy paradigm has been taken to task for advancing a hyper-individualistic image of social life that is both inaccurate and destructive. With roots in the ancient regime of private property, critics argue, the "right to be let alone" has become obsolete in a world of increasing interdependency and dangerous in world needing new recognition of our communal fates (Glendon 1991). And efforts to make sense of what privacy is and what role it should play in today's world have resulted in widely recognized confusion, even chaos, in the legal and philosophical literature (Regan 1995, 3). In the terms of Thomas Kuhn's famous work (1962) on transformations in scientific theory, the privacy paradigm is so beset by anomalies and failures that it may be time for new perspectives and understandings.

The people that we meet in this book put forth an alternative to the standard vocabulary and venue of the surveillance-privacy debate. It is an understanding of surveillance that is tied to the realities of their daily lives and to the powerful forces that shape them. It centers our attention on the conflicts between people's efforts to live and cope and the powers of surveillance to control and punish. And it helps us to understand the broad impact of surveillance programs as frightening and degrading strategies that affect people in ways that may have little to do with the particular behaviors that are the focus of the system. In short, our exploration of these women's lives and words draws forth a critique of surveillance which says far less about privacy and legal rights than it does about power, domination, and conflict. In the chapters that follow, I will argue that such a critique makes sense and, further, suggest that it generates terms and ideas that could help us all as we struggle to understand and confront the politics of surveillance. While it would hardly makes sense to argue that these perspectives could "displace" the privacy approach as a framework with which to think about surveillance, it is well worth thinking about the ways in which conversations about surveillance could be expanded and made more complete with attention to these concerns.[7]

Like the very walls of protection that it seeks to create around the individual, the privacy claim builds walls around our capacity to understand the political—for better and worse, it tries to hide specific and substantive needs and desires behind the "right to be let alone." And because the abstract claim of privacy seeks to hide so much, apply to so many things, and be so universal, our widespread reliance on it promotes a tendency to ignore the specific and very real relations of power and domination that are at work in policies of surveillance. It is my belief that the American conversation about surveillance would be a better, more engaging, and more vital one if we worked to move questions about power and domination to the forefront. In this work, by paying close attention to how surveillance forbids, shapes, and frightens a very real group of American citizens, I hope to contribute to that much-needed refocusing.

Along with listening to what these women say, this work also studies the tension between the experienced everyday lives of the welfare poor and the depiction of their lives that is created by the state's surveillance system. Frequently, surveillance policies are presented as if they merely produce a clear and simple snapshot of reality. But as we confront the chasm between how these women depict their own lives and how the welfare bureaucracy portrays them, we see that a system of surveillance is not just a means of passively watching the world. Bureaucratic surveillance manifests a way of seeing and knowing the world that excludes much of our true complexity while moving a small cluster of characteristics to the forefront. Simplified criteria that are important to the state—such as documentation regarding income, family makeup, or evidence of unreported resources—push aside the other facets, dimensions, and complexities of the lives of the poor. I will argue that a surveillance system is not just a way of watching the world, it is a way of seeing and knowing the world that shapes both our understandings of reality and our capacities for action. Such systems impose an order upon the world with official declarations about what matters and what does not and, as they do this, they shape important decisions about the distribution of rewards and benefits, as well as punishment and costs. In this light, critiques of surveillance that focus just on the "invasion of privacy" may be both misguided and too limited—as bureaucratic surveillance becomes the defining administrative mode of our times, it will be far more important to account for and battle the ways in which one particular and rather bizarre view of the world becomes *the* view of the world that guides policy and politics.

THE MISSING POLITICS OF RIGHTS

Don't clients have rights? I mean we are human beings. They treat you maybe like we are garbage but I think that they forget that we are human beings and we have rights. And we should have rights by the constitution. . . . It's terrible. Let's do something about it. Let's go down there and protest.

Mary

Legal rights claims like those which Mary voices have been at the center of some of the most successful emancipatory and egalitarian social movements of our times. From the African American Civil Rights Movement of the 1950s and 1960s, to the Women's Movement of the 1960s and 1970s, to the Pay Equity Movement of the 1980s, the rights revolution has been a central part of progressive politics in the United States (Epp 1998; Kiss 1997; Silverstein 1996; McCann 1994; Schneider 1986; Scheingold 1974). More topically, the American Civil Liberties Union and other opponents of increasing surveillance have long used rights claims to privacy and due process in their political and legal struggles (Gellman 1997; Gilliom 1994) and the welfare rights movement of the 1960 and 1970s made effective use of rights claims and legal strategies in their struggle to improve the conditions of the poor and the administration of services (Bussiere 1997; Davis 1993).

Often, the images of rights and struggle presented by lawyers, leaders, and media outlets depict rights as political and legal "trump cards": powerful claims to moral recognition that have the capacity to fundamentally shift the nature of a conflict. Mary's stirring assertions that "we should have rights by the constitution" and her call to "go down there and protest" show the power and potential of such an understanding. But Mary is almost the only woman interviewed for this study to make such claims. For the others, as seen in chapters 3 and 4, the promises of legal rights are in some way irrelevant, unreachable, or remote—they simply don't come to mind or take shape as ways to make sense of and act upon this part of their world. Research on the everyday uses of law has raised important questions about just how universal and meaningful "rights talk" and the initiation of legal conflict are as ways of thinking, speaking, and acting about personal and political problems (Engel and Munger 1996; Merry 1990; Bumiller 1988; Engel 1984). All of these studies have shown that there are other ways to frame problems, other venues in which to resolve conflict, or, importantly, that people will ignore or accept problems and injustices rather than speak and act out a politics of rights. Thus, while some authors have depicted a nation of rights-bearing citizens driven by law's universal and abstract system of meaning (Glendon 1991), our status as citizens, our framing of issues, and our thinking about rights and law are far more variable, contextual, and open-ended matters. "'Legal consciousness'" suggest Engel and Munger, "emerges from the continual interplay of law, everyday life, and individual experience" (1996: 14; see also Ewick and Silbey 1998: 34–37; McCann 1994: 283).

For these women, I will argue, the interplay of law, everyday life, and individual experience do not make for a mix in which rights talk is a central theme as they struggle with welfare surveillance. For them, there is no doubting the fact that "the law is all over" (Sarat 1990). The law surrounds them as rules, as threats, and as commands; it is there as police officers, caseworkers, lawyers, and fraud control investigators; it is there in constructing their status as dependents of the state. The law is all over, but, to put it bluntly, rights are not all over. These emancipatory, empowering, entitling elements of our legal system evade the women studied here and rarely emerge in their ways of speaking or acting about their problems. To them, I think, most of what they associate with "the law" is exclusive, threatening, and mean-spirited.[8]

By exploring the context and implications of their rights reticence, I hope to contribute to our reassessment of rights not by advancing another critique or defense of rights, but rather by exploring the promises and possibilities of critique and action which eschew legal rights as their formative principle. What we will see are important alternatives to rights talk in the vernacular critiques of the women studied here. They advance arguments that make sense of the world and lead to agendas of action by centering attention on particular needs that emerge out of daily life and particular actions aimed at fulfilling their needs. While there is clearly much to be lost in the departure from the conventional languages of public conflict, what these claims and critiques based in particular need bring as an alternative to rights is important. What they may give up in nobility, they may gain in accessibility. What they may give up in their capacity to unite and universalize, they may gain in personal relevance. And what they may give up in their potential to lead to widespread demands for fundamental change, they may gain in the realization of short-term and much-needed little gains in the effort to get through the day.

These much-needed little gains in the effort to get through the day are the final topic on the agenda of this work. Here, I refer to the politics of everyday resistance. Everyday resistance encompasses the daily struggles of the powerless as they work with limited resources to fight the powerful as best they can. In a peasant society it means pilfering some grain from the landowner or sabotaging the new equipment that threatens traditional livelihoods (Scott 1985); in formal legal settings it means feigning compliance while rigging penalties so that they create no real burdens (Ewick and Silbey 1998); in a welfare setting it means getting paid under the table, hiding assets, or trading in food stamps in order to make ends meet. Everyday resistance is a form of politics that tends to have little use for traditional ideologies (such as the framework of rights), for traditional strategies (like litigation, petition, or even organized protest), or for traditional movement goals (such as formal changes in government policy). Some scholars of social movements (Handler 1992) have juxtaposed the politics of everyday resistance with more conventional social movement politics and then raised valid concerns about the risks of making too much of the necessarily limited capacities of the everyday resistance as a form of political action. But the findings of the research at hand show that resistant practices are an important dimension of the politics of struggle and that, here at least, they achieve important goals and advance important principles as they affirm the shared and laudable values of responsibility and care in these mothers' lives. In a context of little hope and few resources, I will argue, everyday resistance is a terrain of action that must be taken seriously by students of politics. And, in a political system that seems fundamentally unable to take serious action toward limiting the spread of surveillance practices, everyday resistance may soon be the only form of politics left for those who struggle to check them.

Critics of this perspective may argue that I am celebrating disaster: that my attention to forms of critique which forgo the emancipatory capacity of rights and to forms of action which eschew formal organized politics aimed at the achievement of lasting change is a form of treason against the poor people with whom I have worked. They may argue that just as both the poor and the opponents to increasing surveillance are in most desperate need of organized action, works like this attempt to gild the opposite—that we seek to make something grand out of the daily, tiny, and often quite sad struggles of people in apparently hopeless circumstances. In the way of a preemptive caveat let me say this. The politics of everyday resistance are, by definition, no grand strategy and they promise no grand reforms. But they are, nonetheless, *here*, and they appear to be both widespread and significant in the lives of individuals and institutions, not just among these women but among all the law-bending, radar-detecting, tax-dodging residents of the land. Any complete accounting of political domination and conflict like that studied here should not simply ignore everyday struggle because of a preference for the more conventional politics of formal and public movements.

THE PLAN OF THE BOOK
Chapter One: Welfare Surveillance

Drawing on recent studies of governmental knowledge, on archived original documents, and on scholarly works and legislative reports regarding the history of welfare in the United States, chapter 1 depicts the key dimensions in the history and current setting of welfare surveillance. In the unique design of what would be popularly thought of as "welfare" in the United States, high levels of investigation into the lives of the poor have always been a central part of relief programs. Emphasis on the "means test" (which demands a close accounting of an applicant's resources), on moral assessments about a "worthy home," and on explicit goals of discouraging participation, means that investigations into the lives of the poor have not only been thorough but, generally, designed with little attention to the dignity of the client. During the late 1960s and early 1970s, some of the most abusive practices were curtailed by pressure from activist attorneys, the poor, the courts, and political leaders, but by the mid-1970s a punitive emphasis had returned to welfare surveillance. By the late 1970s, the computer revolution was bringing about the installation of massive and powerful Client Information Systems which, by the time the research for this book took place, had been installed as comprehensive, high-speed systems of gathering and analyzing information about the welfare poor. The chapter closes by framing these innovations within a critical assessment of governmental knowledge and exploring the state's epistemology of the poor.

Chapter Two: Stories of Struggle

In chapter 2, we begin to look at how welfare clients describe and complain about their struggles with the information demands and oversight of the welfare bureaucracy and its computerized systems. The chapter opens with an explanation of how the empirical research for this book was carried out. It is argued that one of the best ways to learn about a hierarchical system of surveillance is to go the bottom of the hierarchy and encourage people there to speak in ways that are normally forbidden. The epistemological and methodological reasoning behind my practice of asking welfare mothers to engage in taped, semi-structured conversations with other welfare mothers is explained. Next, through a series of close-up looks at several of the women, we begin to see the shapes of their lives on welfare, their struggles, and their complaints about the surveillance apparatus. In line with my argument that our most effective means of uncovering the nature of hierarchical surveillance is to give voice to those at "ground zero," the chapter relies heavily on extended verbatim excerpts from interviews.

Chapter Three: Rights Talk and Rights Reticence

Chapter 3 is an effort to make sense of the diverse array of views expressed in the preceding chapter. We focus on the relative absence of the traditional complaints about how surveillance measures invade an existing legal right to privacy. By studying the contexts in which these women live, with a particular emphasis on their relationships with the welfare bureaucracy, we can see that numerous aspects of their condition work against the assertion of rights. As they live in a world that is marked by fear, by dependency, and by poor access to information, it is little wonder that they do not boldly assert their complaints about welfare administration (see also Soss 1999). And as they live with a system of laws that is threatening, confusing, and mean-spirited, I argue, it is even less wonder that an emancipatory vision of legal rights does not spring forth. Turning to engage with recent research on legal consciousness and rights mobilization (such as Ewick and Silbey 1998; McCann 1994; Sarat 1990; Bumiller 1988), I argue that this examination of people who *do not* use rights or even speak rights contributes to the many studies that center on those who do.

Chapter Four: The Need to Resist

Chapter 4 argues that in the place of what might be public protests and the mobilization of rights discourse is a quieter form of politics and a different framing of moral claims. In the place of the traditional argument about rights to privacy is one more closely tied to these women's particular needs as parents and people. In short, they say little about rights and much about family needs. Noting that the emphasis on care and need is deeply resonant with a more widely noted "ethic of care" that has been positioned as an alternative to the more individualistic system of rights, the chapter tries to make sense of the implications of this ethic as well as its apparent emergence as a viable critique of welfare surveillance policies. One of the findings of the research is that most of the women here engage in small deceptions, evasions, and other such acts in order to hide sources of income, extra support, or potentially damaging information from the welfare bureaucracy. Chapter 4 argues that these patterns of secretive struggle are forms of everyday resistance—patterns of oppositional activity that express and mobilize the women's critique of the surveillance system. While some moments of everyday resistance have been skeptically assessed as being individualistic, unprincipled, and largely futile, I will argue that the everyday struggle we see here advances important values, achieves important ends, and both acts upon and reaffirms admirable and widely shared principles of human responsibility.

Chapter Five: Privacy and the Powers of Surveillance

Chapter 5 concludes *Overseers of the Poor* by pulling these various strands into an empirically grounded critical account of both surveillance policies and the ways in which we normally speak about them. Because a central point of the book is that surveillance policies must be understood within the particular contexts of specific lives and power relations, generalizations must be made cautiously and tend to be more about the questions we should ask than about the answers we shall find. Addressing some of the identified drawbacks of the "privacy rights" framework, I argue that the new understanding developed here can contribute to a critique of surveillance practices that is more inclusive, more comprehensive, and may hold greater promise as a broadly relevant framing of the issues at hand. Last, I assert that a retooling of our thinking about the politics of surveillance must fully incorporate questions about power and domination; these critical elements are at the heart of most significant surveillance initiatives but are often sidelined in the mainstream debates.

Epilogue

Finally, an unplanned epilogue to this work reflects on some of the foregoing arguments by offering an account of my own experience as the subject of police surveillance. Through an unfettered personal narrative recounting a police search of our home and my family's subsequent struggles with various suspicions and investigations, I try to explore some of the conditions that unite us all as the subjects of surveillance as well as some of the the broad gaps created by differences in class, gender, and the capacity for legal action.

CHAPTER ONE

Welfare Surveillance

I N THE WINTER OF 1915, the following reports were filed as part of the home examinations required for applicants to the Mother's Pension in Muskingham County, Ohio:

> Mrs. Hooper lives on the top of Owen's Hill in a two story frame house. There are two rooms on each floor. These rooms are scantily furnished but are clean and well taken care of. The house is three stories at the back, but the brick basement has no doors. The kitchen has a door at the back but no steps leading to the yard. The porch was not clean but that is pardonable owing to the very muddy yard and being the only entrance to the home. She has milk from her brother's cow in return for carring for the cow. [*sic*]

> Mrs. Dieter lives with her mother, brother, and two children in three rooms on the second floor of her mother's home. . . . The apartment upstairs is crowded with furniture but [she] is one of the clean Germans and no improvements can be made in the keeping of the rooms. The furniture is plain but good and well kept.

•

In the years of the Great Depression, the family of my Uncle Steve, like most of the steelworker families in Ohio, fell on hard times. Little work was available and many families, including theirs, turned to the government for "relief." Among the rules for receiving aid was that families not have a functioning automobile. Uncle Steve's dad, and other men in the neighborhood, met this requirement by putting their cars up on cement blocks and removing the wheels. When a home inspection was made, the investigator could report that no working vehicle was owned by the family. If a rare trip was absolutely necessary, my uncle's family would put the wheels on and make the drive. But for daily travel, like the nine-mile trek to see if there was work at the mills, the men walked while their cars sat on blocks. If the mills were hiring, the fathers would use part of their wages for the return fare on the electric street car. If there was no work, they would turn around and walk home.

•

More recently, those few applicants for assistance in the state of Ohio who actually read through the many pages of their application and consent form come across the following statement about bureaucratic surveillance and computerized investigations of their financial claims:

> The human services department will use your social security number when contacting people or agencies to obtain information needed to determine your eligibility and verify information you have given. For example, your social security number may be used to check your income and/or employment information with past or present employers, financial resources through IRS, unemployment compensation, disability benefits received from state or federal sources and any other appropriate local, state, or federal agency to verify information you have given. . . . Your social security number, as well as other information will also be used in computer matching and program reviews or audits to make sure your household is eligible for food stamps, other federal assistance programs and federally assisted state programs, such as school lunch, ADC and Medicaid.[1]

To complete their application, they were required to sign a broad series of information-access waivers, capped off by the comprehensive and disentitling: "I give my consent to the agency to make whatever contacts are necessary to determine my eligibility for assistance and to verify information I have given in this application."

These three examples of welfare surveillance, taken from different periods of the twentieth century, allow us to see the points that I hope to make in this chapter. The first, and most simply put, is that welfare surveillance is nothing new. From today's computerized information systems, to the visit to Mrs. Hooper's home in 1915, and back to the surveying and badging of the poor in sixteenth-century Europe, governments have closely examined those who seek assistance.

The second is that the images and understandings of the poor that are created by welfare surveillance are not only strikingly partial, but partial in ways that reflect the political, social, and technological conditions of the era. From the records we learn that Mrs. Hooper's husband has died, that she has a milk supply and a clean two-story frame house, but not if she has significant financial investments or a marketable skill. In the time of Mrs. Hooper and Mrs. Dieter, it was important that the one had a cow and that the other was a "clean German." No mention was made of automobiles, because it was beyond imagination that the rural poor could have one at that point, and no mention was made of computer matching, because computers did not exist. By the time of the Great Depression, computers were still absent, but the existence and condition of the family car was the most memorable facet of a family's brush with the scrutiny of welfare officials. By the 1990s, cars are still recorded in computer programs—and there are caps on their allowable value—but there is no mention of family cows, and a caseworker would undoubtedly face some trouble for recording their impression that a woman was one of the "clean Germans." For the purposes of welfare administration and surveillance, a simplified depiction of the poor must focus on those characteristics which are both observable and deemed to be important in the execution of state policy. The resulting depictions will always reflect the tenors and dynamics of the time as well as the perspectives and capacities of the state. As we watch the terms, practices, and priorities of welfare surveillance shift with the social and political changes that mark the last century, we can see and begin to understand the extent to which the state's vision of the poor is always a product of particular prejudices, assumptions, values, and technical capacities. Understanding the factors that make up these particular emphases is a critical element in coming to understand the politics of surveillance.

But the examples also show, third, that not everything changes. One constant in American welfare surveillance is the emphasis on whether or not a family will be eligible for assistance. At the center of this process is the "means test" which consists of some mechanism for determining if someone is eligible by assessing their needs, their resources, or their capacity to work. Was there evidence of a man or inordinately expensive furniture in Mrs. Hooper's home? Did a family have a working car? Do utility bills and rent receipts, computer sweeps of income or investment records, and birth certificates and school attendance records all verify the information provided by a contemporary applicant? In the pages that follow, we will see that this one constant in American welfare surveillance, reflecting both our faith in the importance of labor and our suspicion that people will do nearly anything to avoid it, is the central point in the ongoing state examination of the poor.

Finally, and this topic is taken up in chapter 2, we see the often quiet efforts of the poor to assert their own control over how the events and conditions of their lives are seen and depicted. One can almost hear Mrs. Hooper explaining away the muddy porch during the February home visit or imagine her hiding a few valuable heirlooms in preparation for the inspector's visit. We can see my uncle's father putting the car up on blocks and sense the tragic absurdity of all those men walking all those miles as part of an effort to make reality comport with the guidelines of relief. And we will see, in the latter chapters of this work, contemporary welfare mothers managing their affairs in ways that make the best of their ongoing scrutiny by the automated systems of surveillance that watch over their lives. As the state struggles to know as much as it can about the poor—and to use its knowledge with critical consequences for poor people's lives—an inevitable struggle over information and perception comes to define the unfolding politics of surveillance.

KNOWING THE POOR

Despite a common tendency to assume otherwise, poor people are a complex lot—"a bloomin' buzzin' confusion" as William James put it, or what Jim Scott calls a "complex and unwieldy reality" (1998, 11). Demographically, "the poor" includes all races, colors, ethnicities, religions, and ages of people, although it is heavy on women and children. Ideologically, there are conservatives, liberals, radicals, and plenty of enigmas. Physically, there are tall, short, thin, and fat. For most of us, "the poor" includes family, friends, students, and neighbors. There are urban and rural and some suburban. The adult poor include those who never stood a real chance in the economy because of location, gender, disease, discrimination, or disability, and there are those who stood a chance, but for some combination of bad luck and personal and social failure haven't made it. Among the poor are also men and women with special talents for music, art, mechanical repair, oratory, hunting, cooking, gardening, and a host of other human endeavors. There are people who are immensely kind-hearted, there are scoundrels, and there are many who, like most of us, struggle between the two poles. And "the poor" shift through time as different people move in and out of the ranks.

In short, those who at some period of time populate the low end of the income distribution scale in the United States are indescribably varied and multifaceted. But for the government to take action with or upon them, they must, as James Scott argues in *Seeing like a State*, be made "legible" or fit into terms, categories, and characteristics that are observable, assessable, and amenable to the management and information regimes of modern bureaucracy (see also Dandeker 1990; Foucault 1979, 191). He argues that "Certain forms of knowledge and control require a narrowing of vision. The great advantage of such tunnel vision is that it brings into sharp focus certain limited aspects of an otherwise far more complex and unwieldy reality. This very simplification, in turn, makes the phenomenon at the center of the field of vision more legible and hence more susceptible to careful measurement and calculations. Combined with similar observations, an overall, aggregate, synoptic view of a selective reality is achieved, making possible a high degree of schematic knowledge, control, and manipulation" (1998, 11).

This project of making the poor legible is hardly a new one. As far back as 1531, British law "decreed that local officials search out and register those of the destitute deemed to be impotent, and give them a document authorizing begging. Almsgiving to others was outlawed . . . [and] for those who sought alms without authorization, the penalty was public whipping till the blood ran" (Piven and Cloward 1971, 15; see also Torpey 2000, 18). Soon after, authorized beggars were required to wear badges marking their status (Handler and Rosenheim 1966). In Britain and colonial America, a public office called "the overseer of the poor" was created in order to monitor the collection and delivery of aid to the poor and keep careful records of their identity and whereabouts. From the sixteenth-century surveys of the poor to the comprehensive computer-based Client Information Systems that most states now use, welfare administration has been inextricably a process of struggling to "know" the poor; to measure, depict, and examine them in ways which both express and facilitate the power and techniques of modern statecraft.

"To Define, Locate, and Purge"

Like any system of surveillance and administration, welfare programs need to simplify the world by focusing on a limited set of factors. In studying the history of welfare surveillance it is patently clear what the focus is on. At different times, though techniques change, one persistent and fundamental question is the bedrock for all of the state's knowledge about the poor: whether or not they are "deserving," "worthy," or "eligible" for assistance. Whether it be the sixteenth-century judgment of economic impotence, a labor test, a woman's status as a widow and worthy mother, a eugenicist's classification of imbecility, an investigator's declaration that a family car is not working, or a modern computer's determination of income eligibility, the center and pivot of the state's efforts to know the poor is the question of whether or not the state will help them.

Michael Katz's *In the Shadow of the Poorhouse* finds early evidence of this pattern in the Quincy Report (1821), a Massachusetts study which divided the poor into two separate categories:

> 1. The impotent poor; in which denomination are included all, who are wholly incapable of work, through old age, infancy, sickness or corporeal debility. 2. The able poor; in which denomination are included all, who are capable of work, of some nature, or other; but differing in the degree of their capacity, and in the kind of work, of which they are capable. (Quoted in Katz 1986, 18)

Katz continues by noting that the view of the Quincy report was that "no one should hesitate to help the first class of poor," and that the "real issue" was the problem of the able-bodied poor. "According to the Quincy Report, all the 'evils' attributable to the current system of poor relief could be traced to the same root: 'the difficulty of discriminating between the able poor and the impotent poor and of apportioning the degree of public provision to the degree of actual impotency.' The able poor, so it was assumed, should fend for themselves. Indeed, it is only a slight exaggeration to say that *the core of most welfare reform since the early nineteenth century has been a war on the able-bodied poor: an attempt to define, locate, and purge them from the roles of relief*" (ibid., emphasis added).

Many weapons have been used in the war on the able-bodied poor, but there appear to be just a few primary strategies. One—seen in the preceding excerpt—is the use of categories which divide the poor according to such distinctions as age, gender, parental status, physical condition, and mental acuity. The very young, the very old, the disabled, or mothers of young children have typically been more likely to receive help. Another very important dividing line is drawn between those who are poor enough to receive aid and those that the legislatures deem wealthy enough to go it on their own. These distinctions among the poor establish lines of demarcation which can be drawn during the deployment of tactics falling under a second main strategy, examination. Examination would include things such as the gathering of basic demographics about a family or individual, administering a labor test, visiting the home, or other means of gathering information with which to depict the poor and ensure that they truly meet the criteria set forth for the awarding of assistance. Third, and often accomplished in the design of the examination, is deterrence. Here, the goal is to make the process of applying for and receiving aid —as well as the more general status of "being on the dole"—so demeaning and onerous that only the most desperate would ever apply. This could range from requiring uniforms, to publishing names, to engaging in exhaustive investigations of poor families.

The strategies of categorization, examination, and deterrence are readily apparent in the almshouse, or poorhouse, era of American relief. As opposed to "outdoor relief," which allowed aid recipients to move about in the community, the "indoor relief" of the poorhouse requires the poor to live within the walls of a total institution, often in uniform, and under strict rules of behavior and mandates of forced labor. By creating a total institution which was the only major source of relief, the poorhouse movement was able to both sort and control the poor and, through the deterrent effect of these institutions, force the poor to sort themselves. As poorhouses began to give way to the more active use of "outdoor" relief, the overseers of the poor turned to different tactics in the effort to test and judge. One was the "labor test" in which poor men would split wood or break rock in an enclosed work yard. By requiring hard and long hours of work from aid applicants, officials could combat idleness, keep the subjects under their watchful eye, and deter those who may be able to find other types of work.[2]

Toward the latter decades of the nineteenth century, the "scientific charity" movement brought new practices to the treatment of the poor and began an evolution that would gradually produce the contemporary profession of social work and the contemporary regimes of welfare surveillance.[3] One of the central principles of scientific charity was the "friendly visitor," a prototype of the modern social worker who would go into the homes of the poor to advise, inspect, support, and instruct. These "visitors were supposed to be both investigators and friends. They were to inspire confidence and radiate warmth as they intruded into the most intimate details of their clients' lives" (Katz 1986, 67). As one leader described the working principles of the scientific charity movement: "The fundamental law of its operation is expressed in one word. 'INVESTIGATE.' Its motto is 'No relief (except in extreme cases of despair or imminent death) without previous and searching examination'" (the Rev. Gurteen, quoted in Trattner 1999, 96).

"A Modern-Dress Version of Poor Relief"

In the late nineteenth and early twentieth century, countless experiments were tried in the nation's programs for the poor. Under the influence of Social Darwinism and the more broadly conservative turn in American business and politics, public sector assistance—never generous—all but died off. Privately funded scientific charity continued, the Community Chest movement began, and with the rise of the Reform Era came the settlement house movement and numerous experiments regarding public health and welfare in different urban areas (see Trattner 1999; Katz 1986; Ferguson 1984, 34). And it was in this period that we see what Linda Gordon calls "the first modern public welfare in the United States": the precursors to AFDC known as the Mothers' Pensions. "State and local governments established programs to aid single mothers, mainly in the decade 1910–20. These authorized assistance to 'deserving' poor single mothers with children, to defray the costs of raising children in their own homes and to deter child labor and the institutionalization of fatherless children. The enthusiasm for mothers' aid was so great that forty-six of the forty-eight states had passed such laws within twenty years. The design of these programs was so influential that when, twenty years later, the depression provided an opportunity to establish a federal program —ADC—it simply added federal funds to the mothers'-aid model" (Gordon 1994, 37).

The Mother's Funds varied greatly by location, but Winifred Bell's research makes it clear that surveillance and judgment were a critical component in many areas, usually bundled under the requirement that children be raised in a "suitable home." Thus "Massachusetts and Michigan specified that no male boarder, other than the mother's brother or father, could live in the home. . . . A number of states defined a tubercular parent as 'physically unfit.' Several states required that the religion of the child be protected and fostered, and, if the mother failed to do so, she was an improper person to have custody of the children. . . . Kansas required that the mother be 'provident'" (Bell 1965, 7–8). And the list goes on. From the types of visitations and inspection seen at the beginning of this chapter, to the midnight raids in search of male visitors, the watchful eye was a central part of almost any assistance to the poor.

It was with the economic collapse of the Great Depression that the modern era of American welfare really began. The omnibus Social Security Act of 1935 (SSA) created a whole series of programs in the area of social welfare. Some, like the old age fund and unemployment insurance, were not cast as "relief" and were less encumbered by stigma and scrutiny (Gordon 1994; Fraser 1989).[4] But in another area—focusing on women and their children—the Social Security Act created little more than a "modern-dress version of poor relief" (Handler and Rosenheim 1966, 379). As noted, under the program called Aid to Dependent Children (ADC, later AFDC for Aid to Families with Dependent Children), the federal government took over much of the financial responsibility for what had been called "mothers' pensions" or "widows' and orphans' funds." These state, county, or township programs had been devastated by the Depression's twin impact of sharply rising need and sharply falling tax revenues. As the SSA brought monetary assistance but little policy guidance, local practices and programs remained largely in place. It was here, in the program for women and children, that the most degrading and invasive tactics of modern welfare would be seen.

Linda Gordon explains that while the original Social Security Act did not mandate that the largely autonomous states undertake intensive surveillance in the administration of the early ADC program, the Social Security Board was encouraging states to do so within just a few years of passage. Describing the board's "model state bill" for 1936, Gordon notes that it "called for investigations of the home and periodic reconsiderations of the amount of assistance. Home visits were the norm in casework at this time, and many social workers argued that clients preferred home visits, to protect their privacy against meeting others or being seen by others. The drive to control expenses soon shifted the locus of supervision to offices, which most clients in fact preferred, and surveillance focused more on receipts and budgets and less on housecleaning. But the assumption remained that a public assistance client was in need of counseling and rehabilitation and had fewer privacy rights than others" (1994, 296).

From these beginnings, the politics of welfare surveillance only grew more and more intense. The dynamics of the transformation are summarized in William Trattner's *From Poor Law to Welfare State:* "Whereas between 1935 and the early 1950s, the elderly received the bulk of federal and state welfare funds, by the middle of the [1950s] recipients of A.D.C. . . . outnumbered all others receiving such assistance. Furthermore, whereas earlier most recipients of A.D.C. were dependent white children with widowed mothers, an increasing number of those who received such funds now were single black women with illegitimate children—a trend that would increase significantly in the following years. Thus, in the late 1950s state after state began instituting punitive administrative policies designed to reduce the number of such welfare recipients and to deter new applicants. State residency requirements were strictly enforced so that migrants (especially blacks moving from the South to the North) would not receive assistance, and all sorts of new eligibility investigations were initiated, including 'suitable home' and 'man-in-the-house' policies" (1999, 309–310).[5] It became clear that the enforcement of the means test and the investigative practices surrounding it were one of the key means through which welfare officials could reduce rolls or meet other political goals.[6]

It is, of course, unavoidable that information gathering and record keeping are part of large-scale public administration—indeed modern government cannot begin to function without constructing elaborate structures of rationalized information (Scott 1998; Dandeker 1990). But because the American style of poor relief places so much emphasis on assessing the capacity of people to fend for themselves and on deterring those who can—through means tests, stigmatization, man-in-the-house rules, labor tests, residency requirements, or the scrutiny of the friendly visitors—it must be even more surveillance intensive than it might otherwise be. As Handler and Rosenheim argued, a "social insurance" system—like Social Security—avoids some of the intrusions seen here because there is "a detailed statutory definition of eligibility, a statutorily prescribed benefit schedule, and, often, a contributory scheme of finance" (1966, 379). Since Social Security assumes need and works with established terms of eligibility and support, case-by-case scrutiny can be minimized, while AFDC, with its emphasis on the individual determination of need, frequent reporting, and ongoing determinations of "worthiness," is driven to engage in some of the most invasive forms of scrutiny imaginable.

The exceedingly invasive aspects of welfare programs such as AFDC and Medicaid are also tied to the fact that they deal with those who would be considered society's least powerful—poor, often minority, women and children. In *Unruly Practices*, Nancy Fraser explores the disparities between the management of entitlement programs such as unemployment and social security, which deal with largely male "citizens," and welfare programs such as Food Stamps, AFDC, and Medicaid, which involve dependent and largely female "clients." She concludes: "The relief programs are notorious for the varieties of humiliation they inflict upon clients. They require considerable work in qualifying and maintaining eligibility, and they have a heavy component of surveillance" (1989, 152–153). In sum, the combined impact of the administrative mode of the modern state, the focus on eligibility assessment, the emphasis on deterrence, and the disdain for and powerlessness of welfare clients, means that the welfare poor are subject to forms and degrees of scrutiny matched only by the likes of patients, prisoners, and soldiers.

THE DECLARATION ERA

In the late 1960s, however, things changed somewhat—levels of scrutiny declined, application hurdles were lowered, and many welfare clients received fuller benefits. In a nutshell, 1969 regulations for AFDC administration required states to experiment with a "simplified" method for determining eligibility. The "declaration method," as it is known, "provides for eligibility determination to be based, to the maximum extent feasible, on the information furnished by the applicant without routine applicant interviews or verification procedures" (Congressional Research Service 1977, 30). For some combination of reasons, including urban militancy, relatively progressive national leadership and local administration, litigation and advocacy by progressive attorneys, the effect of War on Poverty policies, and the impact of mass protest and mobilization, the climate of welfare surveillance shifted during that period. The level of suspicion, hassle, and investigations dropped, as program administrators placed greater emphasis on accepting the terms and condition of poor people's needs as they were presented by the poor themselves. Piven and Cloward wrote that "Traditional procedures for investigating eligibility broke down: home visits were no longer made with any frequency, requirements that forms be sent to various agencies to determine whether the family might have collateral income or eligibility for other forms of assistance . . . tended to be neglected. For all practical purposes,

welfare operating procedures collapsed; regulations were simply ig-
nored in order to process the hundreds of thousands of families who
jammed the welfare waiting rooms" (1979, 274–275).

In *The Fraud Control Game*, Gardiner and Lyman summarize the
transformation in the following words: "During the 1960s, federal
policies encouraged welfare agencies to base AFDC eligibility, as far
as possible, on information volunteered by applicants. Extensive verification was discouraged in favor of increasing agency responsiveness
to recipients and decreasing the extent of intrusion into their personal lives as a requirement of program participation" (1984, 18). In
an important sense, there was a momentary shift in the politics of information, with the poor—at least in some regions of the country—
in the position of advancing their own version of needs and budgets,
their own version of resources, and their own take on the government's "means test." Furthermore, through the work of poverty attorneys, welfare rights activists, and social program workers, it was
frequently the case that *welfare agencies* were the ones subject to scrutiny and sanction. In New York, in particular, there was a focused effort to monitor local offices for rules-compliance, to widely publicize
sources of assistance that the poor might be unaware of, and to provide active counsel to the poor on the ins and outs of living on welfare (Piven and Cloward 1979). The counties of Appalachian Ohio
saw their own version of this transformation in the late 1960s and
early 1970s when community action workers and other activists began training welfare clients on rules and regulations and, frequently,
accompanying them to meetings with caseworkers (author's interviews). It was an important transformation.[7]

QUALITY CONTROL

But it was a short-lived transformation. After "a considerable degree
of controversy," new regulations in 1973 "significantly reversed" the
emphasis on declaration and on the capacity of poor families to depict themselves (Congressional Research Service 1977, 30).[8] The end
of this experimental period in welfare administration came amid
the decline of the broader African American protest movement, the
fracturing of the welfare rights movement (see chap. 3), and the 1972

triumph of a Nixon campaign that had made welfare a key issue in speeches and advertisements (Piven and Cloward 1979, 332). Tellingly, the Nixon administration signaled its more punitive and conservative approach to welfare through intensified scrutiny of the welfare rolls and enhanced surveillance of both clients and state-level human services bureaucracies.

The "Quality Control" (QC) movement was one of the most important federal policy catalysts for the resurgence of fraud control efforts and related practices of surveillance at the state level. Although the beginnings of the QC program can be traced to the early 1960s, it was really in the early and mid-1970s that the federal government's efforts in this area began having a significant effect on the state and local administration of welfare. The 1973 QC regulations included stiff financial penalties for states that failed to meet federally stipulated rates of accuracy in case administration. These first penalties were ruled unlawful by the courts in 1975. But by the late 1970s Congress had reworked the legislation with a series of financial penalties and incentives designed to produce state compliance with target goals for error reduction. As the federal government intensified its scrutiny of state-level AFDC administration by closely reviewing samples of cases, many states began intensifying the scrutiny of their AFDC clients, frequently shifting from income estimates to mandated monthly reporting and beginning the use of computer matching and other means of more closely inspecting their clients.[9] By the early 1990s, the Quality Control movement was so well entrenched that a new verb entered the vocabulary of welfare caseworkers and administrators: to be "Cue-ceed" (QC'd) was to have a case or caseworker's files pulled for review by the audit division (author's interviews).

Since the 1970s, there has been a consistent and dramatic expansion in the extent and sophistication of welfare surveillance in the United States. Politically, these changes were fueled and capacitated by the increasingly conservative climate in the nation. From Nixon, through Carter, and then particularly through the Reagan and post-Reagan years, the "right turn" in American politics has been dramatic. And, as might be expected, conservative politicians did not have a lot of love for the poor or the programs that supported them. President Reagan's attacks on mythical "welfare queens" drinking vodka in their

Cadillacs were only the most bizarre and extreme of the attacks on America's neediest. As in the past, the more punitive orientation toward the poor put increased surveillance of the welfare rolls at the top of the agenda for welfare administration. In 1977 President Carter and HEW secretary Joseph Califano undertook the highly publicized Project Match as a demonstration of the capacity of computer matching to ferret out welfare fraud. The same year, Congress mandated the use of "wage matching" in AFDC administration and sidestepped the largely toothless Privacy Act of 1974 by giving states permission to access Social Security and other data files regarding the income of American citizens (Greenberg and Wolf 1986, 19–20). By the early 1980s, President Reagan had established his Council on Integrity and Efficiency to undertake a "Long-Term Computer Matching Project" intended to facilitate and improve the use of computer matching and related techniques in federal and state government (ibid., 19).

Other changes and dynamics helped fuel the expansion of information gathering and control. Beginning in the mid-1970s, AFDC administrators began to pursue more seriously the child support payments that many "deadbeat dads" (and a tiny fraction of deadbeat moms) had failed to pay. Since AFDC clients were required to sign these monies over to the state, these collections emerged as an important budget item and pulled the welfare agencies into great efforts to establish paternity and pursue child support. By the mid-1980s, federal guidelines required that states attempt to establish paternity. County welfare offices were holding monthly "blood draw days" in which dozens of children were called in to be DNA-typed so that the state could try to identify their fathers (this gave way to saliva-based tests in more recent years).

Today, almost any welfare application triggers a referral to child support enforcement agencies who work, if necessary, to establish paternity and pursue support. Women who refuse to identify sexual partners when paternity is in question can be ruled ineligible for benefits (author's interviews). In important ways, it was as if the notorious man-in-the-house searches of earlier years had returned in a more complex and contemporary form. Until the late 1960s, AFDC administrators in some areas of the country had undertaken midnight or early-morning raids to see if an unreported male was present in an

allegedly single-parent home (Handler and Rosenheim 1966, 381–
383). These old-fashioned searches were struck down by the courts,
but now the search for the man extended beyond the walls of the
house—using tools ranging from DNA analysis to the tracing of Social Security numbers in the numerous state and federal data banks,
the men were being searched out wherever they might be.[10] The transition from the door-crashing search for a "man in the house" to
the high-tech tracing of "absent parents" is an apt metaphor for the
broader transformation in the nature and design of welfare surveillance. A tradition of personalized supervision has given way to forms
of technological surveillance and bureaucratic control that may be less
face-to-face but are certainly no less pervasive or controlling.

THE CLIENT INFORMATION SYSTEM

. . . because a machine can do it better than a worker.
        John Dempsey, director, Michigan Department of Social Services

I have it *all!* [laugh] But he was very upset that I even knew
anything.
                                AFDC caseworker, Southern Ohio

As with the workplace drug-testing movement of the 1980s (Gilliom
1994), the contemporary changes in welfare surveillance came about
through a fusion of political climate and technological innovation. In
this case, the computer revolution made possible, for the first time,
comprehensive sweeps of huge bodies of data on mainframe computers. Later, the spread of networked desktop computers made it possible for individual caseworkers to be directly connected to the results
of those sweeps. The computerization of welfare administration also
enabled states to compile their entire caseloads into comprehensive
statewide systems, to compare their caseload to that of other states
and programs, and to evaluate the performance of individual caseworkers or particular work units. In short, computerization brought
an unprecedented level of bureaucratic transparency to welfare administration and facilitated levels and types of surveillance that were
simply impossible under previous technologies.

The politics of welfare administration are almost indescribably complex. With some federal funding and guidance, some state funding and guidance, and some local funding and guidance, welfare administration is a chaotic federalism or, perhaps, simply chaos. Although states differ in how they run their AFDC programs, the general scenario is a poorly paid caseworker, in an office or cubicle in a local welfare agency, in the context of a county system, under the guidance of a state-level department, taking leadership from the state legislature, the Congress, the courts, and the federal bureaucracies. Needless to say, guidelines and directives, from whatever the source, are unlikely to flow smoothly through the system (Gardiner and Lyman 1984). Further, before Client Information Systems (CIS) revolutionized welfare administration, immense physical barriers were created by an administrative and record-keeping system based entirely on paperwork and oral exchanges. Because of this, the older systems simply precluded much in the way of cost-effective scrutiny and review of local performance. Gardiner and Lyman describe it as "organized anarchy" (1984, 55) and Florence Zeller's 1981 study of efforts to reduce AFDC overpayments argued that the welfare system was "so much like a Chinese wooden puzzle" that the effects of actions or techniques could not even be assessed. Unless, that is, there were "major changes, *such as a computer system*" (1981, 84–85, quoted in Gardiner and Lyman 1984, emphasis added).

It is for these reasons that the CIS movement was such an important change in welfare administration. Simply put, the CIS brought a revolutionary degree of administrative centralization and transparency to a previously confused and jumbled mass of administrative back streets and dark alleys. In the span of a few years, all state records were moved onto statewide systems capable of managing and manipulating huge amounts of information. A direct link was established between a caseworker's decision—entered on a terminal linked to the CIS—and state-level administrators. And those state-level administrators could easily examine rates of error or case problems occurring in the county, the office, or even a particular caseworker's desk.

CRIS-E

In the state of Ohio, where this study is based, the new Client Information System was first dubbed CRIS and, later, CRIS-E, for

"Client Registry and Information System—Enhanced." Bureaucrats and caseworkers pronounce the name as "Chris (pause) E."; a respected person with a protected last name. Clients pronounce the name as "Crissy"; juvenile and disliked. However one chooses to pronounce its name, CRIS-E is an electronic system of surveillance and administration with immense powers for information management. It creates a statewide network that links each caseworker's terminal to a main system containing the complete files of every client. As explained below, the CRIS-E system works with the Income Eligibility Verification System (IEVS)—the program encompassing most of the regular computer number matches—to provide caseworkers and administrators automated access to all federal and state number matches.[11] CRIS-E also offers an on-line intake program, in which a program known as "the driver" leads caseworkers through a screen-by-screen interview of welfare applicants, then calculates eligibility and, if appropriate, authorizes the issuance of emergency assistance.[12]

The advances in surveillance, as measured by sheer apprehension and possession of information, were immense. The list of factors loaded into the system covered, among other things, veteran status; living situations; household income and expenditures; age, names and Social Security numbers of children; health information; work history; marital status; race; criminal history; divorce history; medical insurance; savings and checking accounts; burial contracts; cemetery lots; life insurance; Christmas clubs; and retirement plans. The lists go on to include unearned income and queries about alimony, dividends, union pensions, worker's compensation, black-lung benefits, and any "money from another person." And always, at the end of every list, "anything else?"

The data cover costs of telephone, sewer, garbage removal, electricity, and gas. CRIS-E wants to know if you are on strike and, if so, for how long. If you work, the driver wants the job title, the hourly rate, and the monthly hour totals. It will also ask whether there are aliens in the home, if there are people needing long-term care, if there are any pending insurance settlements, and if there are any changes in the household income or composition expected in the near future. One study at the county level concluded that a typical client would be likely to encounter about "770 questions related to her personal and financial circumstances" and that regulations covering these topics cover over "4,300 pages, with another 2,000 pages of clarifications" (Athens County Department of Human Services, in-house study). And all of this information is logged onto a single statewide computer system, bringing the welfare poor of Ohio into one massive digital poorhouse—each and every one of them easily visible to the new overseer of the poor.

The easily accessed statewide filing cabinet created by CRIS-E has obvious relevance to the sort of information panopticon discussed in the literature on surveillance systems (see, among others, Foucault 1979; Dandeker 1990; Gilliom 1994; Zuboff 1988; Gandy 1993). It places the roughly three-quarters of a million aid recipients in Ohio into one electronically created site in which all relevant data regarding their lives as recipients are stored and easily accessed. The extent to which this transforms the system cannot be overstated.[13] Previously the time and space obstacles to case management and client control were insurmountable; paper records were in thousands of filing cabinets spread out across Ohio's eighty-eight counties. The possibilities for centralized surveillance and control were sharply limited by the simple facts of physical distance and the resulting information fragmentation in the system.

But the screens and software of CRIS-E have replaced the file cabinets, the long application form ("the book"), the manual arithmetic of caseworkers, and much of the rule-finding and interpretation involved in case administration until the late 1980s. With pencil, paper, and file cabinets now far from view, caseworkers fill out application data, calculate benefits, and maintain client records in a system that can be accessed by any caseworker or administrator in the state. Further, the computerization of the state's aid administration means that a wide spectrum of state and federal computer matches can be rapidly and automatically processed. Bringing in data from the Internal Revenue Service, the state's tax office, the Social Security Administration, worker's compensation, and a number of other state agencies, the computer matches use clients' Social Security numbers to see if they have told the truth regarding their needs and resources.[14] The IEVS matches (IEVS is actually only one part of a broader array of matches, but the term is used within agencies to refer to all of the matches available) have, according to at least one county Director of Human Services "revolutionized" the detection system: "We catch a lot more people. In fact, we'll get any kind of legitimate income" that a client may be receiving. With the major exception of underground income, IEVS does appear to have revolutionized control within the agency.[15] The Department of Human Services (DHS) no longer takes the passive pose of waiting for a rat call.[16] The bureaucrats, with their massive computer system, are able to monitor most forms of legitimate income that occur within the United States. As one interviewed caseworker explained: "Before IEVS we couldn't pin down what our clients were doing without the aid of anonymous phone calls or just client admissions that they had been working. [Now] we get monthly alerts on IEVS matches. Anybody who's been in the system for ninety days, we start getting matches on. So right off the bat we are catching more of our clients lying quicker."

Suddenly whole new capacities for gathering and using information entered the daily practice of welfare administration. An AFDC caseworker (BJ) who was interviewed by the author as a part of this project explains one client's surprise:

BJ: This gentleman here was very upset with me when I first got
       his case. He demanded to see me because . . . I had sent him
       out a form. . . . We got this thing [a computer match alert]
       showing that he had received workman's compensation. I
       sent him a letter telling him that I had received information
       that he is receiving workman's compensation [and that he]
       needed to update his information so that I could add it to
       his case. He got *highly* mad at me. He came in here and de-
       manded to see me and demanded to know *how I knew* that he
       was getting workmen's compensation. And I couldn't show
       him the screen, I'm not supposed to let him see the screen—
       I don't know why because it's his information and they can
       watch us go through the application—so I didn't show him
       the screen and when he did give me [the document with] the
       information he crossed *everything* out. He was so upset that
       he would not let me see anything off of his workmen's com-
       pensation paper, he took a black magic marker and [crossed
       out] everything because he didn't want me to know his claim

number or anything else. I have it *all!* [laugh] But he was very
upset that I even knew anything.
How did you resolve it?

BJ: I told him, I said we just get alerts, I said we get information
through the state with Social Security, unemployment, anything like that. And so he turned the information in to me;
he was just upset that I knew it and could find it out without
him telling me. And after he realized. . . . I wanted to show
him the screen so bad. He probably thought it was just words
and that I couldn't do it. 'Cause before I couldn't've, and if
they've been on assistance for a very long time, they probably
thought I couldn't and [that] they could hide information
from me.

Conclusion: An Epistemology of the Poor

Forms of knowledge and bodies of information are *always* particular
ways of seeing the world, with particular premises, agendas, omissions, and genealogies. In chapter 2 we begin to look at the particular
forms of knowledge found among the welfare mothers who are the
subjects of these information and surveillance systems, but here the
focus has been on the systems of welfare surveillance themselves and
how they must be understood within the context of broader patterns
of meaning in our approaches to poverty. At the center of welfare
thinking—and so much else—in the United States are the ideas of
patriarchal individualism and the market. The premise of welfare
administration is that the normal state of affairs consists of male-
headed, two-parent families earning food, shelter, and clothing by
obtaining wages through labor in the economy. In a program like the
Mother's Pension or AFDC it is upon failure in terms of this model
—the male dies or leaves and the woman and children become "dependent"—that the state provides assistance. With constant hope and
suspicion that all could be "independent" (that is, for the most part,
dependent upon an employer or male wage earner) and live on their
own means, the state constantly searches for traces of resources, earn-
ings, and even signs of "a man in the house" or, now, a "man in the
nation."
    Adjacent to the specific ideological premises of welfare adminis-

tration and surveillance is a broader philosophy of knowledge—an epistemology, or way of thinking about what information and knowledge is. The world of welfare surveillance is state-centered, bureaucratic, and rationalist. It is a world of facts, errors, verification, and evidence. Legislatively stipulated figures for eligibility, support levels, and other dimensions of the program are provided, documents, forms, and receipts are gathered, and determinations are made. It is only with a radical leveling or simplifying of the state's understanding of the poor that the necessary uniformity and simplicity of the automated computer information systems can function. We have seen that for a brief time, prior to the era of computerization, the declaration period in AFDC experimented with giving clients a central role in stating their need and situation, but for the most part the poor exist as objects in the system. There is no voice for the poor in the establishment of levels and criteria (and support levels in most regions of the country are widely known to be inadequate). There is usually little voice for the poor in making the case for their need—documents, receipts, and formulae assert it for them. Scott argues that it may be essential for the welfare state—broadly conceived—to view the social terrain in this way:

> Officials of the modern state are, of necessity, at least one step— and often several steps—removed from the society they are charged with governing. They assess the life of their society by a series of typifications that are always some distance from the full reality these abstractions are meant to capture. . . . The functionary of any large organization "sees" the human activity that is of interest to him largely through the simplified approximations of documents and statistics: tax proceeds, lists of taxpayers, land records, average incomes, unemployment numbers, mortality rates, trade and productivity figures, the total number of cases of cholera in a certain district.
>
> These typifications are indispensable to statecraft. State simplifications . . . represent techniques for grasping a large and complex reality; in order for officials to be able to comprehend aspects of the ensemble, that complex reality must be reduced to schematic categories. The only way to accomplish this is to reduce an infinite array of detail to a set of categories that will facilitate summary descriptions, comparisons, and aggregation. (1998, 77)

As the historical examples have shown, government agencies have been struggling to know and depict the poor for a long time. Welfare surveillance is certainly nothing new. But the technological transformation brought about by the emergence of the CIS, automated case management, and the capacity for computer matching marks an important shift in the breadth and depth of the state's capacity for knowledge as well as its capacity to apply that knowledge in the execution of policy. Parallel to the society's broader revolution in the capacity and implementation of surveillance technology, welfare surveillance has hit new levels of quality and density. It has constructed a world in which there is little room for secrets and even less room for arguments over basic values and knowledge claims.

These changes, not just in welfare, but in consumer marketing, taxation, drug law enforcement, educational assessment, and the other institutions of our lives, are important social and political transformations. They mark not just an increase in the technical capacity for observation but an increasing reach and force for centrally determined norms, standards, and values. As we experience an unprecedented extension of the institutional power to enforce these norms, we experience a concomitant reduction in the capacity and power for self-definition in our lives. The welfare mother, the health insurance consumer, the taxpayer, the student, and the loan applicant all have different lots in life, different agendas, different needs, and different resources. But they all unite in being increasingly subject to these new systems of power.[17]

It has been argued that much of the activity surrounding the production and use of knowledge in welfare administration is part of a broader mission of keeping the welfare rolls down through detecting or deterring those who could possibly do without. Although there are clearly numerous other purposes in the information quest of welfare surveillance—such as matching clients with appropriate programs, identifying particular needs, or intervening in crises—the central and most enduring mission appears to be that of what the modern bureaucracy calls "eligibility verification," that is, limiting and controlling access to welfare in the ongoing skirmishes of what Katz called "the war on the able-bodied poor" (1986, 18).

As the poor struggle to find means of survival, a struggle over the politics of information necessarily ensues. Programs of scrutiny are designed to augment the hassle, intimidation, and humiliation of applicants with an eye toward the policy goal of deterring all but the most desperate from seeking aid. Specific tactics within programs— the poorhouses, the uniforms, the surprise home visits, the invasive questions—align with a broader cultural shaming of the poor in the mass media to create barriers to anyone asking for help. Politicians make frequent attacks on "welfare fraud," and as their widely publicized results both stigmatize and frighten the poor, application levels decline. For those who ask for and receive help, of course, the barriers are no longer barriers, but ongoing punishment for their plight. The poor, normally hampered by a partial and unsure knowledge of the complex system, by low education, and by fear, struggle to advance and maintain a version of their "case" that makes the most of the possibility and level of aid. The state, hampered by a partial knowledge of the poor and cumbersome layers of bureaucracy, struggles to assert its control and detect violations of the order. But the state's arsenal against the poor has gotten a lot more sophisticated in recent years.

CHAPTER TWO

Stories of Struggle

In my semi-annual visit to this home I found the home as clean
and the mistress as cheerful and brave as at my last visits.
                    Mother's Pension Inspection Report by Emma G. Martin,
Assistant Probation Officer, Muskingham County, Ohio, June 20, 1917

We must never assume that local practices conform with state
theory.
                                        James Scott (1998, 49)

THE PRECEDING CHAPTER argued that the contemporary client information and surveillance system of the welfare bureaucracy exemplifies the reductive and authoritarian ways of knowing that mark
modern bureaucracies. These systems of knowledge are organized by
and for centers of power—they are "state ways of seeing" that place
a premium on efficiency and convenience for the execution of policy and systematically deny local and personal forms of knowledge or
unique claims of particular people or contexts. There is ample evidence to conclude that these systems of surveillance and analysis are
more than mere research tools for the human services bureaucracy;
they are themselves forms of domination which overrun personal depiction, contextual variety, and particularity. The subversion of these
limited and necessarily flawed ways of knowing is an important element of the pages that follow. To understand the nature and impact
of a surveillance regime we must study what the system silences—
the people, perspectives, and practices that the official depictions are
blind to and those which must be hidden because the rules forbid

them. Through coming to know the everyday practices and patterns of activity that take place in these blind spots and back alleys of a surveillance system, we can begin to build an empirically grounded critical understanding of the ways that modern surveillance affects our lives and our world.

To do so, we will, in many ways, invert the normal format of welfare surveillance. Here, it is the state that will be largely silent, while the poor speak. It will be poor women explaining their own experiences from their own vantage points, rather than providing documentation to prove that they meet the criteria of centrally determined formulae. It will be the poor who provide the language with which to think about surveillance, need, and the welfare bureaucracy, not the bureaucrats, their lawyers, or their cohorts in the academic world. Authoritarian surveillance is by definition a form of knowing which discounts, excludes, and objectifies the subjects of its gaze. To truly confront it as a form and edifice of power, we hope to reverse the rules of the game and assist the discounted, excluded, and objectified in telling their own tales.

The Research Project

It is fairly easy to find people who are subjected to intensive surveillance—surveillance policies are simply so ubiquitous at this point that one can throw a stone almost anywhere and hit a subject of sustained monitoring and analysis. A typical worker, for example, would face the ongoing surveillance related to policing, taxation, and consumerism, but also such things as workplace drug testing, performance monitoring and evaluation, and other forms of observation, measurement, and analysis. A typical student would also face the background surveillance of policing, taxation, and consumerism, but may also have academic testing, dormitory searches, athletic drug testing, and the general scrutiny of university life. A credit card user or World Wide Web traveler undergoes constant assessment and analysis as often unseen systems record and apply information about their habits. Most people live with surveillance as a regular part of their lives.

But some people live with surveillance as a totalizing and encompassing force which can critically affect their well-being. It was this sort of people that I hoped to study, and although there are many that could be imagined—parolees, military personnel, professional criminals, and others—I settled on the welfare poor for a number of reasons: One, certainly, was proximity and accessibility, since I live and work in the rural Appalachian region of southeastern Ohio, a region with more than its fair share of poverty. Another is that welfare is an area of administration with a long history of surveillance and of scholarship interested, at least in part, in the experiences of the welfare clients who participate in the system (Edin and Lein 1997; Edin 1993; Polakow 1992; Sarat 1990). Yet another reason is that in the course of the late 1980s and early 1990s, the welfare poor in Ohio, and many other states, underwent a dramatic intensification in the scope and density of the surveillance in their lives.[1] As new and comprehensive computer systems enabled levels of scrutiny that would have been unheard of in previous years, the welfare poor of the early 1990s found themselves coming to terms with wave after wave of new programs and portfolios of information. In short, they began to achieve the dubious distinction of being subjected to some of the most sophisticated and intensive monitoring devised.

Today's welfare surveillance is a system of defining, implementing, and enforcing the law through which individual cases are evaluated and responded to in terms of predefined categories, in which centrally defined norms are asserted upon a complex, large, and dispersed group of people, and in which violators of the codes are actively sought out in regular computer number matches, telephone hotline programs, and other other control measures. It is here that we find the most tangible source of conflict between the poor and their overseers. Because the design of a system like AFDC requires families to fit closely defined categories of income, status, and need, and then remain true to those categories to continue receiving aid, welfare clients are uniformly pressured to present a version of their lives that maximizes their potential for support. And because the level of cash support under AFDC is well below a livable income, clients are also uniformly pressured to seek additional income which, necessarily, must be kept secret. Further, even if income would be allowed (which it often is), the complexity, obfuscation, and informal security surrounding the actual terms of welfare rules mean that clients can rarely be sure whether they really need to hide what they hide, so they do so as a necessary precaution.

In sum, the welfare program studied in this project could almost have been designed to ensure ongoing struggle between poor families and the welfare bureaucracy—the direct interests of the former push them to manage information about their case as effectively as they can, and the legal and political mandates of the latter push them to detect each little departure from the truth or the norm.[2] Any withholding of information or misrepresentation of facts regarding the makeup, resources, or income of the family is a violation of code, and the information systems for modern welfare are specifically designed to catch the poor in these misrepresentations and petty crimes.

The welfare poor of southeastern Ohio, where this study is based, also have the dubious distinction of being what is perhaps one of the most powerless groups in American society. The people studied here are women who are mostly on their own as heads of households in a region with little in the way of support, infrastructure, or economic opportunity. They live in a time when it is almost a crime in itself to be poor—when state and national politicians build careers by degrading and assaulting the poor and removing or weakening support systems. They also tend to be poorly educated, limited by the gender and class expectations of the region and the broader culture, and isolated from networks of support or organization.

Southeastern Ohio is often called "the other Ohio." Its geography, its forests, its small farms, and its abandoned coal mines make it far more similar to its close neighbors of eastern Kentucky and western West Virginia than the state lines would have us think. Falling into the federal government's Appalachian region, the area continues to suffer under the forms of endemic rural poverty and underdevelopment that have marked the region since the nineteenth century (Halperin 1990; Caudill 1963). It is the sort of place where young families face a very high likelihood of turning to various government programs for assistance. And when they turn to these programs, though they never leave the hilly and forested terrain of the region, they enter one of the most sophisticated information panopticons of modern governance.

Design of the Study

In many ways, the research design of this project was defined as much by what we *couldn't* do as by what we could. We could not work through welfare agencies because, as discussed earlier, among our central interests was coming to know what the agencies cannot see or what they would forbid if they could. There is simply no way that the level of autonomy and trust needed for this sort of research could be achieved using agency rolls or facilities as a means for contacting the welfare poor. Mass survey instruments, often used in an effort to learn about people's views, also seemed inappropriate. We were, by definition, hoping to learn the kinds of things which cannot be pre-coded into a formal survey instrument, and we suspected that we would be learning about practices which anyone would be a fool to document on a form.[3]

In the end, we settled on the sort of in-depth semistructured interviewing technique that a number of recent works (McCann 1994; Ewick and Silbey 1998) have used as a practicable blending of the sort of deep and closely situated knowledge of a full-blown ethnography and the broader, more generalizable knowledge of survey designs. In this study, given the particular hope to explore local everyday knowledge by giving voice to poor women's stories about complex and deeply personal issues and potentially criminal activity, we decided to attempt a kind of self-telling. Two local women, both recent former welfare clients, agreed to serve as paid project consultants and field interviewers.

Working through local interviewers had a number of advantages. For one thing, the field interviewers had a thorough firsthand knowledge of the region, of life as a woman in poverty, and of welfare, and they could use their own stories and wisdom as part of a conversation. We also hoped that the shared gender and social status, as well as the notable accent of the region, would help to establish a quicker relation of trust and more complete sharing of perspectives and practices. Finally, we were trying to break away from the established academic discourse about surveillance and the law, and this approach to the interviews guaranteed much more distance from the world of academe —a distance which could help the local voices emerge. After some

training on interviewing practices, the goals and design of the research, basic questions to be covered,[4] and terms to be avoided, the
field interviewers set out with tape recorders in hand to undertake
one- to two-hour interviews with AFDC clients spread over four
counties in the Appalachian region of southeastern Ohio.

A number of challenges confronted us in identifying a "sample,"
that is, who it is we would talk to. Obviously, sampling could not be
done through a welfare agency master list because an affiliation between our study and the Department of Human Services would put a
damper on client willingness to talk candidly about their experiences.
Given these concerns, we opted for the "snowball" sampling that
Kathryn Edin (1993) has used so successfully in her research of urban
welfare families. The field interviewers began their interviews doing
"practice runs" with a few welfare mothers that they already knew.
Each of these interviews concluded with a request for a few names
of other people around a four-county area and for permission to
mention the first subject's name in a personal introduction to those
people. The people named were then contacted and, if appropriate
and possible, interviewed. Those interviews, in turn, concluded with
another request for names, and we quickly developed a diverse collection of people living in different parts of the region. In the end, we
spoke with forty-eight mothers from a four-county area.[5]

While such an approach raises obvious concerns for those seeking
samples which could be certified as "scientifically representative," the
more important goal here was to find access to the welfare poor of the
region in a way that would offer the level of trust necessary to undertake meaningful interviews about topics which might include illegali-
ties. Once individuals were identified, contacted, and had signed a
form consenting to participation, they were asked to assign themselves a pseudonym which we then used for the rest of their contacts
with the study. At no point in the study was it possible to link a particular woman's interview to her true name and identity except, perhaps, through the recollection of the field interviewers themselves.[6]

The interviews begin with some basic information about the
women and their families and turned, as something of an "icebreaker,"
to ask subjects to tell the story of how they ended up going on public assistance. We asked how they were "getting by"—how far their

check and food stamps took them and what they did when they ran out.[7] We then sought to probe their level of satisfaction with the service and treatment they receive, the nature of their relationship with their caseworker, and the extent to which their caseworker provided ready information about policies and procedures. The interview then typically moved to gauge the client's level of knowledge about welfare surveillance. What did they think the computer files contained about them? What did they think that computer matches were capable of discovering? We also asked questions about what the client did to "earn a little extra money" or "make ends meet." We asked how they felt about these activities, whether or not they feared detection, and what other people they knew did in this vein. Following this, the subjects were informed of the system's actual surveillance capacity, and we moved into a discussion of their feelings about the scope and nature of the verification system and how such a system would affect the different types of income enhancement that clients engaged in. Finally, we asked them if the interview had raised any concerns or questions and, if it had—and it frequently did—the field interviewers did their best to address them as well as provide references to potential sources of help such as legal services or a local welfare official known to be sympathetic.

As the Mothers See It

This section centers on five women's perspectives on welfare surveillance—Mary, Shawana, Sally, Eliza, and Marilyn. By taking a focused look at how they perceive it, criticize it, live with it, and subvert it, we can get a tangible foundation for the more general discussion that follows.

Mary
You got to make it somehow.

Mary lives in southern Ohio, is in her early forties, and has three children living at home. The family has been receiving AFDC benefits, food stamps, free school lunches, child care, and Medicaid for about three years. Unable to find full-time work and aware that she "didn't have any kind of skills to get a good job," she is attending school to improve her prospects. The fathers of her children pay child support, but the Department of Human Services keeps all but fifty dollars a month to offset the cost of her benefits.

After talking about the types of support Mary received, Karen, the interviewer, asked Mary about the first time she applied for welfare. The conversation quickly turned to the complex forms, questions, and demands for documentation:

> M: Well, they want too much. I mean, they have to know every time you breathe, and you are afraid to do anything because they will find out about it. . . .
> K: Why do you think they need to know all this stuff?
> M: To see if you are eligible, I guess. . . .
> K: In terms of all the documentation they have on you, do you think if you took a job somewhere, maybe not in [this] county, but outside of [this] county, that they would be able to find out about you working?
> M: Oh yes, [by] my Social Security number, I would imagine.
> K: What about if you had a savings or checking account in a bank here or in another state?
> M: I think they could.
> K: What about unemployment or disability?
> M: Yes, I think they could.
> K: How would they find this out?
> M: Through my Social Security number and a computer. I don't know, but I always thought they could, and I don't want to go up the creek.

After stating that no one can "make it on their benefits alone" (see also Edin 1993), Mary said that while she had never worked a side job, she did receive assistance from family members. She then goes on to explain things that other ADC clients do to get by and to argue for the morality and necessity of what they do. It is an explanation seen in slightly different forms among many of the interviewees.

> K: Do you receive any kind of assistance from anybody like family members [or] the children's fathers?
> M: The children's father buys gifts for them and things. But I found out that was OK, or like if I go to him for school clothes. I've learned how to get around the system so to speak.
> K: How do you do that?

M: By having him buy them clothes. I go to the store with him and tell him what they need and he will buy it for them. . . . If I take money I'm in trouble—he could get me in trouble later on. But if I take gifts then I know I'm OK.

K: Do you know anyone else who receives ADC?

M: Oh yes.

K: Do you know if they do anything to get around the system?

M: Yeah. Because you could not make it with what they give you. I know lots of people that are working and drawing ADC. Like one of the ways this one girl is doing it is that she's working at this job and . . . they give her a check, but that isn't the right amount of money. . . . Then they pay her the rest underneath the table and that is how she makes it, and she only has to turn in this real low check showing what she gets to welfare. . . . But if you work for a place like I was working for, they are not going to do something like that for you. But small town people will try to help you out. I remember when this guy would let me take my food stamps and buy diapers or soap or something like that. Because you can't, I mean, I don't buy whiskey or anything, but you can't make it if you can't buy your diapers and your laundry soap and things. . . .

K: What other kinds of things do people do in terms of trying to make their ends meet?

M: [Babysitting]. . . . I don't think that there is anyone that isn't cheating. But I don't mind a little bit of things like that, but when a guy lays on the couch, and draws it, he doesn't deserve it. You know, when he is able to work or something. . . .

K: How do you feel about doing things the way you do it in terms of having your ex, your child's father buy stuff so that you can get around the system or knowing that other people are getting paid under the table?

M: Well, I'd rather not have to do it but you got to make it somehow. I mean the kids have to have [things] . . . and I only have $421 for four people. That just don't cut it with the rent and utilities and you know they don't allow you anything for any kind of bills, that's for sure.

The explanation Mary gives for why she and others struggle to augment their meager assistance check is simple: she and her children need the money. It is an ethic of survival and the obligation to care for her children. Like other mothers interviewed here, life on the welfare system compels them to resist the demands of that same system by coming up with more money. The welfare agency, in turn, spends millions of dollars trying to prevent them from doing so. One of the biggest new innovations, explained earlier, is CRIS-E, and we asked clients what they knew about it. Mary describes the computer's knowledge in the almost apocalyptic terms used by several other mothers—it knows "everything."

    K: What do you think the computer knows about you?

    M: Where I live, everything about me, everything about my children, everything about me. Where I worked before, I imagine they know it all.

    K: How do you feel about that?

    M: It's not right. I have nothing to really hide, but it's just I don't think it is right that they have to know everything about you instead of just your income part.

    K: What do you mean by it's not right?

    M: Well, I just don't think they should have to know everything. But like I said, they have you over the barrel. If you don't turn everything in you don't get the check. So it's that simple to a client. They know that if they don't do it they don't get any income and whether it is right or wrong, you are just out. So you do what the system says to do. You kind of follow along.

Mary later mentioned that she had once been called in for an unanticipated and unscheduled recertification of her eligibility for benefits. The unscheduled recertification frightened her not only because her case would receive close inspection but because it meant that some unknown event like a "rat call"—an anonymous phone tip alleging welfare fraud—or number match had triggered the inspection.

    K: You mentioned that you have had to come in . . . out of sequence for recertification because you feel that someone turned you in for something. What happened? . . .

    M: . . . You get awful scared because you think, "Oh, is there anything I haven't told?" or "who's got it out for me?" or "who's jealous of me?" because if people get jealous of you or whatever, they will make up things on you and then you could

have your check taken away just because someone told something on you that wasn't even true, you know.

K: When you have had to go in for these meetings when you
don't feel it is your recertification time, say you were just re-
certified last week or last month, you have had to come in
again and fill this paper work out, how do you feel about that?

M: I don't like it. I have to go and dig up all those papers again,
but what else can I do? I won't get my check if I don't do it
again. She made that quite clear. I would be just cut off, but
yet she wouldn't tell me for what reason. And don't you think
that they should have to tell us why they are doing that to us
instead of just be able to do anything that they want because
you need that check? . . .

K: And how does that make you feel?

M: Dependent. You have to watch every step like you are in
prison. All the time you are on welfare, yeah, you are in
prison. Someone is watching like a guard. Someone is watching over you and you are hoping every day that you won't go
up the creek, so to speak, and [that you will] get out alive in
any way, shape, or form. You know, "Did I remember to say
that a child moved in?" "Did I remember to say that a child
move out?" And "Did I call within that five days?" You know
. . . making sure all the time. . . . It's as close to a prison that
I can think of.

This exchange leaves little doubt that welfare surveillance is a significant force in this woman's life—a source of tangible fear, worry,
and dependency that leaves her feeling as if she were in prison. And
Mary has little choice but to yield to the power (they have you "over
a barrel") because her assistance would be cut off if she did not comply. Furthering the tension is the caseworker's refusal to explain the
reason for the inspection—keeping the client in a position of uncertainty, ignorance, and fear.[8] Blinded client, inspecting state, threat of
lost benefits or even prosecution—it is hard to imagine a more compelling example of the politics of vision and how surveillance works
as a form of domination over welfare clients. Within that context
of domination, however, is an emergent pattern of resistance; even as
Mary says that they have her "over a barrel," she begins to reveal the
many ways that clients struggle against the power; she is able to get

around the system by having someone else purchase goods; other people babysit for unrecorded and unreported cash. Even in the face of one of the most advanced systems for the detection of financial activity, we begin to see that the subjects of the system find little ways to sneak something by and, in so doing, to challenge the state's command that all be known.

Shawana
It was a pretty messed-up day.

Shawana is in her mid-thirties. She is married and has three children. The family has been receiving assistance for about three years since an injury left her husband unable to work. The family receives AFDC, food stamps, and Medicaid while she is attending school through a jobs program. When asked how she felt about the documentation requested when she first applied for welfare she said:

S: It was immense. Terrible. It was overwhelming.

K: Did you have any difficulty coming up with the information?

S: I believe I had to come back a second time—seems like I forgot something with all that I had to bring and I had to come back again.

K: Why do you think they want all of this information and documentation on you?

S: Probably for fraud.

K: How do you feel about it?

S: Well, at first you feel like it's quite an invasion. At first I felt like . . . they were suspicious anyway to want so much. But after a while you sort of get used to it.

K: Why do you think they would be suspicious?

S: Well, like the Republicans in now, you are made to feel, you wouldn't want anybody to know that you are on welfare, you know. So I guess even at the sign up process, maybe that deters people from signing up.

K: Why do you think they would want to deter people?

S: . . . to save money.

K: How do you feel about that?

S: It's a shame.

K: Can you explain a little bit more how you feel?

S: I think it is terrible. You don't want to go sign up anyway, contrary to popular belief. You don't want to live that way. It just perpetuates the whole bad feeling that you have when you go. They want all that documentation. I signed up in [an urban] County and it was sad. In fact the day I signed up, there was a real nice looking couple in there. You could tell that the man was a professional and had probably lost his job. You could tell that it was really humiliating for him . . . it's a huge building and some of the element in there is a little intimidating or frightening . . . yeah, it was pretty, a pretty messed up day.

After saying she thought that the welfare department had "a computer network" that could discover a host of wrongdoings, Shawana confessed that she kept unreported bank accounts for her children (theoretically, these should come up on the IEVS match which uses IRS form 1099 dividend and interest figures) and that she made some extra money by babysitting.

S: I babysat for about three months. It was horrible. I wouldn't do it again. But I didn't report that. She gave me about $40 a week for her little boy. And I didn't report it and it was kind of scary.

K: Why didn't you report it?

S: Because at the time we were getting $421 a month. The rent for our house was $350. We just needed that little bit more.

K: Do you know of other people who are receiving ADC benefits who do anything? This is not a question to get you to narc anyone out.

S: I know that. Probably small things like babysitting or maybe even Avon. I really don't know.

K: In talking with other people that you know who are receiving the benefits, have they shared any information with you like I babysit for cash or mow lawns. . . .

S: No . . . you know, you just don't tell people. . . . You just don't know. They could tell someone else even innocently and somehow it could get to your caseworker.

K: What do you think would happen?

S: Well, I'm sure that you would be either kicked out of the program or fined or something.

K: . . . [I]f you were receiving your cash babysitting money, do you think they would be able to prove that if somebody reported you?

S: Well, I guess they wouldn't be, but you wouldn't want your
    whole case brought into inspection anyway, you know.

And, like others, she is deeply torn over what she does, but comes back
to the reality of her need:

S: [It] makes you feel . . . like you are ripping them off. Like
    you are a thief.
K: Do you feel that your babysitting that you didn't report
    and your bank accounts—do you feel that you are ripping
    them off?
S: Yeah, to an extent. I try to live honestly and that is sort of a
    contradiction, a contradiction to myself, but I'm not will-
    ing to tell them the truth about that. . . . You know I don't
    think about it very often, but talking about it makes me feel
    pretty bad.
K: Do you see any need to do anything differently?
S: No. . . . [It's] for my survival.

Shawana is aware of and frightened by the different types of surveillance and monitoring in her life. There is, first, the fear that the
caseworker will find out that she is babysitting. Related to this is
the fear that someone else will discover the arrangement and that
the word will get out in her small town and eventually get back to the
agency. In expressing this concern she raises an issue that came up in
several other interviews—that clients fear other people turning them
in as much as, if not more than, they fear the high-tech computer system finding them. This demonstrates the extent to which new forms
of surveillance are a layering over or continuation of older patterns;
the rat call was the time-honored enforcement mechanism prior to
computerization, and all the fancy technology has not rendered it obsolete. Finally, even though she doesn't think they could prove anything regarding cash-paid babysitting, Shawana explains that "you
wouldn't want your whole case brought into inspection anyway." But
why no fear of the computer network that constantly scans her life?
After the interviewer explained the extent of the computerized surveillance program, Shawana said that she hadn't heard of it, and when
asked how she felt about it, she said,

S: Well, you know, it's . . . the penalty you have to pay for get-
    ting the benefits. You hear about fraud cases here and there.
    People ripping off the system and maybe that's why they do it.
    But after you are on it, you become just sort of numb about
    things like that.

K: Does it bother you, though?

S: Not too bad.

But when the interview came back around to her children's bank accounts—which could be detected—Shawana grew anxious but adamant:

K: Technically the fact that you have bank accounts in the names
    of people in the household, those are considered resources that
    you are really supposed to report. How do you feel about not
    reporting them?

S: I feel bad but pretty defiant about that.

K: Can you explain what you mean by defiant?

S: Well, I started those with just a little bit and they each have
    just a little over $100 and I will keep saving up for them. I
    don't have much to give them. . . . I'd like to gradually get off
    welfare and . . . send them to college some day.

K: So it's their kind of like a college fund. And if the welfare de-
    partment would make you use that?

S: I'd sign it over to my parents. I wouldn't give it.

K: You would move the funds and put it in somebody else's name?

S: Yeah.

K: How would you feel about having to do that?

S: Pretty angry.

K: Why would you feel angry?

S: Because I am not spending it. I'm not gaining from it. For
    goodness sake, it is for three little minor children.

Sally
They are going to punish you either way.

Sally lives with her three children and is in transition, moving off AFDC but still receiving food stamps. In the past, she has used AFDC, food stamps, and Medicaid. Her husband does odd jobs and sells ille-gal drugs. She first applied for welfare when she and her husband were

nineteen, unemployed, and expecting their first child. Given the age
of her oldest child, Sally's first application must have been in the late
1970s, prior to the intensification of fraud control measures. Sally re-
calls that they asked for birth certificates and Social Security numbers
and that it "wasn't that hard."

But she thinks things have changed "these days"—when asked if
she thought that the welfare agency could find out if she had a job or
money in the bank, she said there was a "good possibility." Cindy, an
interviewer, asked her how.

> S: I think the welfare department can find out anything they want
> to find out simply because the computer systems all over this
> nation are all interconnected. You punch your Social Security
> number in. I mean, I think they can find out anything they
> want to.

She then explained that

> Most people that I know that want to stay on welfare and want
> extra income take a job that pays under the table and doesn't
> . . . have checks or check stubs that can be traced or pay Social
> Security or whatever. . . . My husband often did jobs on the
> side for which he got paid cash which I wouldn't turn in, be-
> cause I kept all of the money and the welfare check in order to
> pay the bills and do what needed to be done with the kids. And
> if he wanted spending money he had to find his own. And some
> [other people] are not divorced and supposedly they won't re-
> port that they are living in the same household when indeed
> they are and there are two with an income or at least one with
> an income. [They] give false addresses . . . or say children are
> living with them who aren't.
> C: . . . Why do you think people do that?
> S: Why do I think people do that? Some people do it in order to
> survive financially because you can't hardly have a decent place
> to live and make ends meet on a welfare income. So some
> people do that in order to make life livable. Sometimes people
> do it abusively. I've seen it done that way as well. How I feel
> about it depends on the situation.
> C: If people are doing it so that they have enough money to take
> care of their family how do you feel about it?

S: I think they have every right because they are doing what they have to do to survive.

Cindy, the interviewer, went on to explain the computer surveillance system and asked Sally how she felt about it:

S: It's a conflicting feeling. I guess I feel like it's necessary that they do that because I know there are people who do exploit the system, but personally I've tried very hard not to and I don't appreciate being questioned.

C: You said that some people who are not giving them complete information are doing it to take care of their family.

S: Right. Which is why I said there are conflicting feelings. I feel some people have the right to cover up if they have to, but there are other people out there who are abusing it. And, I guess unfortunately, I guess you have to check everyone. I don't know.

C: They want to see if they can catch you?

S: Unfortunately, I think they catch as many who are trying to take care of their family as they do who are abusing it. But they don't show any discretion. They don't care.

C: They don't care about what?

S: They don't care whether you are doing it to survive or not. They are going to punish you either way—they can strip everything away from you and leave you hanging.

C: What else can they do if they catch you, do you know?

S: I really don't know what all the repercussions are. I don't want to know.

C: Do you think that if people knew that they had this computer system that can do this, would it make people quit doing things to make extra money?

S: Just the fact that they know it? No. If it is their survival mechanism—you are still going to do what you have to do to survive. It is not going to inhibit you. And if it is someone who is abusing the system, well, what keeps a robber from robbing again? He knows he takes a chance on getting caught and it doesn't stop him.

Eliza
It just makes you crazy.

"I just had a baby and I was seventeen and I didn't have nowhere to live so I went to stay with my mom. And I couldn't very well stay there with her and with the baby, I had to help them some way, and that was the only way I knew how to help."

This is how Eliza explains why she first went on welfare. Eleven years later, at the time of the interview, she is married with four children. She never finished high school. Now, her frequent seizures mean that she can neither work nor drive and that her husband must be around the house to help care for her and the children. Over the last few years, she has received a varying combination of support from AFDC, SSI (Supplemental Security Income), food stamps, and Medicaid. After one of the region's frequent floods destroyed their belongings, the family also received cash grants from the Federal Emergency Management Agency (FEMA) and the Red Cross. Eliza took great pride in showing Cindy the furniture and clothing that they had been able to buy. In her story, the poverty, her children, her seizures, and the care that her husband must provide weave together with the impact of the flood and her ongoing struggles. Asked about the documentation that was required to apply for and receive assistance, Eliza says:

> E: I can see their point on wanting to know who you are if they are going to help you. It sometimes can be a big problem to get them papers together, though. Like I got six people here. I have to have birth certificates for six people and Social Security cards, and a lot of times that is tough to get a hold of, especially after the flood. I lost everything in the flood. And I just didn't have it. . . . I had to go back up to the place where you get the birth certificates and death certificates and redo it again and pay $7 apiece for them. And that's not easy to do when you haven't got the income.
>
> C: What about the other kinds of information, you said they wanted things that proved who you are. How do you feel about doing that?

E: I don't know, I guess that it's just, it's actually just a bunch of crap. Because if you go through it all, taking everything in there that they ask of you in the first place, and they are telling you they need more and more, by the time you get it in you are run so ragged [and] somebody is calling your name from the office there and you are just sitting there. You are so worried about everything going around in your mind, you know. All the problems and everything. You try to sort everything out. And a lot of times it just gets all full, and I don't know, it just makes you crazy.

C: Why do you think they want so much information and documentation?

E: I'm not real sure.

C: Have you ever thought about it?

E: Not really.

C: Any ideas?

E: No.

C: Did you ever ask anyone at the welfare office why they needed so much information?

E: No. I try to stay out of trouble with them. I try to do my part. If I have to go in for my interview and stuff, I do that and I just keep everything going smoothly for the kids. I just do what they want me to do. That way I don't get into any trouble, because I can't afford to lose the medical card or the food stamps or anything with the kids.

C: Do you think asking questions might cause problems?

E: Probably.

C: Why do you think that?

E: When you got somebody working in there that's got a lot of things and they just have a better life and sometimes they act like they are giving you this money themselves, taking it right out of their pockets and giving it to you. Sometimes they can make you feel that way.

C: Are you talking about the caseworkers?

E: Yeah, and sometimes even the receptionist will look at you like, "could there be anything lower on the earth than you?" And I don't think that is right. I don't think people should walk in and give them a problem, but I don't think they should give other people a problem. You know they are just there. I

mean nobody really wants to go there for help, and ask for
help. Nobody does. Well, maybe some people do. I have never
wanted to. Like with me: I can't have a driver's license; I'm
disabled, so I can't not ask for it because it is what is keeping
my kids alive and puts a roof over our heads and food in our
mouths.

C: How does that make you feel when the caseworker or receptionist acts like that?

E: It makes me mad. It makes me feel like they are something
better than I am. And you can get to feeling that way and convince yourself that it's the truth. If you have been through it
so much. It don't come hard to convince yourself you are what
they are treating you like. After so long.

Later, Cindy asked Eliza whether she ever withheld information
in dealing with the welfare office.

C: Have you ever kept any kind of information from your worker?

E: Oh yeah.

C: For instance, what?

E: I had someone living with me once and he lived with me and
my family. And he just needed some help at that time and I let
him stay with us and he got on his feet and he was gone. But if
I told them about it they would have changed my food stamps
for sure. I don't know what else they would have done.

C: You think they would have cut your food stamps?

E: Yeah. I can't have them cut. Like I said. I just do what they want
me to do and then I know that everything is going to be OK.

C: Did you ever not tell about other kinds of income?

E: No.

C: That's it?

E: Well, wait a minute. I went to help my aunt clean up a house
and she made some money and she gave me some money for
helping her, so yeah, I didn't report that. So that's probably
about $25 and I didn't report that. . . .

C: Do you know other people that do things to help make ends
meet where they don't report the income to the worker?

E: Oh yeah. I mean it's like if you can do something, a job or
something for somebody that is not going to take you very
long. It's not a hard job, it's not something you have to really

exert yourself into really bad. I mean every little penny counts when you don't have it. And when you get it and you have something like a birthday coming up for your kids or something and you just don't have the money for that birthday present. If something comes up that you can get the money, that's what you do. It's not something that you think, "oh, I should call and tell them about this." Because that money probably went on the whole present, you know, all the money. So it really didn't get any more, it just gave a birthday present.

C: How do you feel about not reporting or how do you feel about others who don't report income or other things?

E: Well, I think if you are doing it to get by, and as long as it's not hurting anyone, you know, you aren't killing anybody or anything like that, I don't see anything wrong.

Marilyn
I hate to lie and defraud anybody,
but there comes a time when you have to.

Marilyn reflects the ambivalence that many of the women feel—in her interview, she is open about the fact that she has kept information from the state and engaged in patently criminal activity in order to support herself, yet she is supportive of the state's efforts to detect and deter people who abuse welfare. She told us that she was on welfare for more than eighteen years while she raised her children and that she now got Social Security for herself and support through AFDC for a grandchild that she is raising. After meeting with her, the interviewer noted that Marilyn "looks like a poor person, looks tired. [She's] only about thirty-seven or thirty-eight but [she] looks tired, worn and sick. She has tumors in her throat and has back problems."

C: Why did you go on welfare?

M: I got pregnant, I was six months pregnant and hadn't seen a doctor or anything. I got on welfare so we could pay for the doctor.

C: So you could get the health card?

M: Yeah, and it helped me out on my rent. I had to eat right.

C: When you first applied for assistance how did you feel about the welfare office's request for documentation of things like your rent?

M: That I can see. I can see where they would have to have all them papers saying how much I spent here and that I was pregnant. They could see I was but I still had to have it, the documentation. I went to the doctor first before I could get the welfare.

C: So you had to have a doctor's statement that you were pregnant?

M: Right.

C: [And do they ask you for birth certificates and other documents?]

M: Every time. I don't think you should have to bring it in every time. They have it on file and you know, like I say, but after [the first time] . . . I don't think you should have to bring them in all the time.

C: Did you have to do that?

M: Yes, every time. . . .

C: Why do you think the welfare office wants so much information and documentation?

M: . . . Probably to make sure you are not lying. You are not trying to fraud them. But they do pay out a lot to different people. . . .

C: Did you work at all when you were on welfare?

M: No.

C: What if you would have been working in a different county, think they would have found out?

M: I don't think they would have found out.

C: Why not?

M: They were in another county.

C: How would being in a different county make a difference?

M: Well, especially if you didn't use your own Social Security number. You know, they couldn't have found out. I think.

C: Have you ever known people that ever did that?

M: Yeah, I have. Plenty of them.

C: Do they work very long doing that?

M: No, not really. Just a little bit. I guess to get their bills caught up.

C: Did you know anyone who got caught doing that?

M: Yes, my ex-husband's wife did.

C: What happened?

M: She has to pay it all back. She got jail time. Thirty days I think for frauding them. Because she was living with a man. He was working and she wasn't turning that in and then she got to working too. They had two kids on welfare. And they had to pay everything back. . . .

C: So you know people who fraud to get bills caught up, have you ever done anything like that?

M: Yes I have, I have lied to the welfare about a man living with me and him working. Because like right now at this time I'm two months behind on my bills. I'm on Social Security now, but still, you know, you can't keep making every payment that has to be paid on that welfare. You can't.

C: Besides having someone living there, anything else that would have gotten you in trouble?

M: No.

C: Did you ever get caught doing that?

M: No. Usually I try to be pretty honest with them because I hate to lie and defraud anybody, but there comes a time when you have to.

C: You said it was to get caught up on your bills.

M: A lot of us do. They talk to me where they are a month or two behind and if you don't get that paid it's going to be turned off and the welfare [agency] won't help you get it back on.

C: You said you hate to lie too much, how does this make you feel?

M: I don't like it, I don't like it at all. When you get asked how many is in the house. So I put down one or how much income and I put down mine and not his.

C: You said that others do it to keep their bills caught up.

M: And they do the same thing.

C: Tell me more about how it makes you feel to have to do that.

M: It makes you feel like a dog. To lie in order to make it month to month. It makes you feel like a low life.

Marilyn's ambivalence is striking. She understands that many welfare families need to make extra money, yet supports state efforts to detect and punish such activity. She "hates to lie too much" but does it, and, as we see here, does other things in her struggle to get by.

C: Since the new computer, have your benefits been easier to get?

M: Yes it has, like I only go in once a year instead of going in twice a year. I don't have all the forms to fill out that I did.

We go in and she asks me and she puts it down on the computer, I sign the paper when she is done. And that is all it is.

C: How about your check and food stamps? Do they come quicker or are there more problems?

M: They are just the same.

C: You mentioned that the computer uses the Social Security number; what kinds of information do you think the computer has?

M: They can do your medical, my taxes and all that, and where you work. All kinds of stuff.

C: Anything else, do they have other information about you and your family?

M: They have everything. You can just punch in that one number and everything would come up, that's the way I feel about it. . . .

C: Do you think this will keep people from cheating?

M: Yeah, a lot.

C: Do you think people will find ways to get around it?

M: They will always find a way around the system.

C: Like how?

M: I don't know, but it seems like they always do . . . people always have . . . they have to make their living. They can sell drugs, not be taking them, but be selling them and be making money.

C: Do you know anyone that did that?

M: Yeah, yeah, I did it for a while.

C: So you could have enough money?

M: Yeah.

C: Did you ever get caught?

M: No.

C: Does it bother you that the welfare office does this kind of checking up on people?

M: No, I think it is about right. They do help you. They try. It ain't their fault if you don't get enough. Look how many people's on welfare. My goodness. It ain't their fault.

TALKING ABOUT SURVEILLANCE

Shawana is initially *just sort of numb*, but then, *angry* because of her children. Sally resents the distrust—she doesn't *appreciate being questioned*. She needs to *survive*, but feels that *they don't care* and will punish her either way: *strip everything away* and leave her *hanging*. Eliza is hassled—six people, a flood-ravaged home, and demand for complete documentation before she can get help—*it's actually just a bunch of crap . . . it just makes you crazy*. She does what she has to do *to get by*. Marilyn *hates to lie*, but *there comes a time when you have to*. It makes her feel *like a dog*. But, in the end, *people . . . have to make their living*.

These are just a few of the diverse stories from the large and complex population of welfare poor in southern Ohio. They include formerly middle-class women trying to escape violent relationships as well as second- and third-generation welfare mothers who had their first children while in their teens and are grandmothers in their mid-thirties. They include mothers of small children, desperately struggling to keep their kids out of what many described as the very poor day care services available to them and mothers of teens who can't find a place in the limited economy of the region. They include women who desperately need all aspects of the support system provided by the human service programs and those who would seem to be most in need of health-care coverage under Medicaid. They include the remarkably articulate and loquacious as well as the taciturn.[9] Some are very conscious of the scrutiny under which they live, others say that they "don't think about it much," though other parts of the interview suggest a sharp awareness. They include women in their early twenties and women in their late forties. Some lived in aging mobile homes with sections of particle board for flooring, others lived in newer and clean apartments or houses. Some looked old beyond their years, alarmingly thin with missing teeth and an air of permanent exhaustion and defeat at the age of thirty-five; others were excited and looked vibrant with energy at the new prospects that lay before them. There were those who were eager to talk about their experiences with welfare and those who simply couldn't fathom our interest in such a boring topic.[10]

In many ways, there is so much diversity that catch phrases like "the welfare poor" are, even if used as a shorthand, categorizations that belie the true complexity and particularity of the population. If they are defined as such a mass, we focus on just a few aspects of their lives—the combination of poverty and the receipt of one type of state aid—at the expense of knowing the true complexity of the many lives we seek to understand. In short, categorical definitions of the "welfare poor" which define them only by their relationship to the state ("welfare") and their economic status ("poor") depict a too simplistic and state-centric understanding of the diversity and challenges which mark these many lives.

This is not to say that there are not important shared conditions of being poor and on welfare—these *are* after all, defining aspects of this group of people [11]—but that those particular aspects are not the only facets of their lives and that we often lose touch with the diversity and self-portraiture that exist amid state-defined groups. What are the patterns amid this diversity? The only ones that are perfectly consistent are the ones defined by the terms of the sample: they are all women, they are all mothers, they are all lower income, they all live in the same depressed region, they are all receiving AFDC (or had done so until shortly before the interview) [12] and some combination of the related social programs, and they are all, therefore, subject to the advanced surveillance of the welfare bureaucracy. In addition to all the diversity we have seen, then, they are all women with children who share a condition of need and find themselves under the high-tech scrutiny of the modern state.

Not surprisingly, given these shared conditions, some widely shared perspectives and issues emerge in the ways that they speak and act about their situations. Some of these are virtually universal to the group: their understandable inability to comprehend the massive and confusing rules of the welfare system, their situations of profound need, and their fear of sanction or reprisal for a violation of the rules. These stand out as conditions which seem to mark almost everyone studied here (and they are discussed in the next chapter). We were also, of course, trying to learn something about these women's views on the impact of surveillance on their lives. Although several expressed pleasure with the extent to which CRIS-E speeds up the processing and delivery of their services, there was pervasive dismay with the surveillance and information demands of the system. But the ways in which they express that dismay vary greatly. As we saw, many talked about how it conflicted with their need to survive or care for their children; others resented the distrust; some focused on personal dislike for officials; another was not consciously critical, but clearly had concerns, since the situation made her "feel like a dog." Most of these conversations touched upon numerous points, with their concerns shifting with the emphasis of the conversation and only taking on any clear meaning within the context of those conversations. (And it is for this reason that this project uses such extensive excerpts and eschews the sort of word counting or categorization that is so tempting in contemporary analyses.) [13]

The bulk of our conversations about welfare surveillance centers on the degradation and hassle of constant scrutiny and the ways in which the scrutiny that these women live with makes it more difficult for them to care for themselves and their children. Their critique of surveillance puts forth an important alternative to the traditional emphasis on the individualistic privacy rights of the abstract citizen, as it puts issues of family, care, and need to the forefront of concern. From their conditions and vantage points as mothers and needy people comes a new voice in the ongoing debate over surveillance policy—one which often sidesteps the legalist terrain of privacy, due process, and rights, and plants itself squarely in the world of everyday needs and concerns. The exploration of this point is a major theme of chapters 3 and 4.

In nearly all these stories, the women have violated the rules, particularly by doing things to bring in a little extra money. Typically, these are their secrets—the things that they need to hide from sight in their struggles with the rules and restrictions of the welfare system. With mixtures of defiance, fear, pride, guilt, and anger, they told us about their everyday struggles to scrape up a little extra cash, or use food stamps for diapers, or hide resources which might threaten their eligibility. As explained in chapter 1, such struggles and subterfuges are almost guaranteed by the combination of the means-test approach to eligibility and the clearly inadequate levels of support provided by AFDC—very few people could be eligible for aid *and* make it through the month on welfare without such measures. As discussed at length in chapter 4, the pervasive and often spirited nature of these everyday tactics marks a humble and widely successful pattern of opposition to the surveillance mechanisms which seek to detect them, define them as fraud, and sanction the offenders. In this way they testify both to the remarkable power and impact of an advanced surveillance regime—because there are so many fears, so many limits, so few hiding places—and to the incredible combination of need and resilience among the target population—because they continue to struggle both because of and in spite of the regime that dominates their lives.[14]

CHAPTER THREE

Rights Talk and Rights Reticence

I don't like everybody knowing me too good.

Marilyn

Don't clients have rights? I mean we are human beings. They treat
you maybe like we are garbage but I think that they forget that we
are human beings and we have rights. And we should have rights
by the constitution. . . . It's terrible. Let's do something about it.
Let's go down there and protest.

Mary

MARY IS ONE OF THE WOMEN we took a close look at in the preceding chapter. She is typical of the other clients in that she is a
single parent of three children who has been receiving food stamps,
cash support, Medicaid, free school lunches, and child care assistance
since she could not find employment with necessary health benefits
about three years ago. She is also typical in that her monthly AFDC
check of $421 runs out well before she finishes paying for the rent,
the utilities, gas and insurance for the car, and clothes for her children. Because of the monthly shortfall, Mary and most of the other
women interviewed for this project engage in what the state would
call "welfare fraud." In her case, she took in an unreported boarder,
decided not to report significant financial help from her family, and
found a merchant who would take food stamps for nonfood essentials
like diapers. She is not exactly sure what the penalties of such law-
breaking would be, but she worries that she could "lose [her] check"
or even "go up the creek." Mary is also representative of many of

these women in her anger over the constant surveillance manifest in the paperwork, documentation, computer number matching, and case reverification involved in keeping her benefits.

In the quotation that begins this chapter, Mary gives voice to her frustrations about surveillance and the welfare system. As she speaks, her words turn more and more toward what we would call "the discourse of rights" or, more simply, "rights talk" (Glendon 1991). In the interview itself, her language grew increasingly legal (and loud) as she grew increasingly angry with her situation and the welfare system; by the end, her "constitutional rights" had been "violated" and she was ready to "go down there and protest!" Mary's words show the promise of a politics of rights (Scheingold 1974). She gains a vital public vocabulary with which to speak about her frustration and anger, linking her complaints to broad and noble traditions of entitlement. She also gains powerful symbols of justice and gravity—the "constitution" is on her side. Importantly, she also sees an action plan —to go down there and protest. Mary, in sum, sounds a lot like a classic example of mobilization around a politics of rights.[1] She also sounds a lot like many participants in ongoing debates over surveillance and information policy—Americans who use the language of rights to privacy when confronted with new tools of monitoring and investigation.

But Mary stands alone. In these one- to two-hour conversations about welfare administration, surveillance, and client information policy, no one else turned so clearly to the language of rights in expressing their widely shared anger and frustration. For most women, rights claims were simply absent; for some, they were were a passing reference. This absence is particularly interesting because, as noted, the prolonged, if sporadic, controversy over surveillance policy in the United States has been particularly defined by claims and conflicts over legal rights to privacy and due process (for examples see Gilliom 1994; Flaherty 1989; Westin 1967).

Here the appeal to rights is strikingly rare. Neither the language nor the actions of these women reflect the sort of rights consciousness or tactical uses of law identified in other studies of people who have grievances, voice them as rights claims, and, perhaps, take some form of legal action. This finding is important both for our study of surveillance and the right to privacy, and for ongoing efforts to learn about the broader politics of rights in American society. On the surveillance front, I will argue that the paucity of claims to a right of privacy and the absence of actions based upon such claims, juxtaposed to the concomitant vitality of alternative critiques and actions, suggests that we should undertake a closer examination of these alternatives in order to explore their relevance and importance as ways of speaking and acting against surveillance programs. With the silence of privacy rights we may be able to hear alternative terms and perspectives with which to confront the powers of surveillance. The bulk of this exploration takes place in the following chapter. In this chapter, I explore the conditions which seem to push these women away from the language of rights.

To do so, we must look to the contexts in which these welfare mothers shape their stance as subjects of the bureaucracy, surveillance, and the law. We will see that they have been stripped of formal privacy rights claims by signing an encompassing waiver in the "consent" form that was part of their multi-page application. Further, federal court decisions and congressional action in the 1970s and early 1980s removed almost any limits on state surveillance in administering welfare programs (see, among others, *Wyman v. James* [400 U.S. 309 (1971)], in which the Supreme Court approved mandatory and warrantless home inspections for welfare clients in New York). Along with the absence of supportive courts or texts, we will see that the women here also lack the sort of activist or activist-attorney presence often seen in the emergence of rights-based movements. Laws, courts, and activist attorneys have been identified as important elements in shaping a turn to rights, translating grievances into the more formal terms of the law (see McCann 1994; Davis 1993).

But it is most critical, I will argue, to study the more everyday interactions and relationships between these women and the welfare bureaucracy (see also Soss 1999). Here, we will see that they live in a context defined by understandable confusion and ignorance about basic regulations, by fear of the welfare agency and its enforcement of those regulations, and by profound need for the support that the welfare system provides. Welfare mothers live in dependence on a system which threatens them with sanction while cloaking itself in complex and poorly explained regulations. The result is that, although they live under an almost totalizing system of laws, they are unable to use other, more emancipatory elements of that same legal system to give voice to their frustrations.[2] It is little wonder that they do not make bold statements about their rights.

Once upon a time, Mary's appeal to rights may not have sounded so lonely. For roughly a decade, from the early 1960s to the early 1970s, activist lawyers worked with welfare clients to advance a politics of rights in the American Courts. Ed Sparer, Charles Reich, Robert Cover, George Wiley, and others, working through the National Welfare Rights Organization, the Legal Services Program, and the Center on Social Welfare Policy and Law created a unique moment in American law. Attorneys from the nation's most elite law schools worked with indigent clients using the appellate courts to enforce and create legal rights for welfare clients and often winning important victories. Charles Reich wrote of giving welfare benefits the protected legal status of a property claim, and activists spoke seriously of creating a constitutional right to food, housing, and income.

Important victories were racked up before the United States Supreme Court. In *King v. Smith* (329 U.S. 309 [1968]), the Court prevented states from cutting off AFDC benefits to children under the "substitute father" or "man in the house" policies which held that any male present in the home assumed responsibility for the support of the children (or, in other moments, that having a man in the house made it an "unsuitable home" which was therefore ineligible for benefits). *Shapiro v. Thompson* (394 U.S. 618 [1969]), argued twice before the Court, struck down state requirements that welfare recipients reside in a state for a given period of time before achieving eligibility. *Goldberg v. Kelly* (394 U.S. 254 [1970]) ordered that welfare benefits could not be cut off without a hearing in which recipients could confront charges against them. In so doing, the Court took a strong step toward Reich's new property arguments that "welfare assistance is a 'legal entitlement' to be administered in accordance with 'due process of law'" (Bussiere 1997, 152).[3]

In subsequent cases, however, the tides began to change. Although some important victories were achieved in the early 1970s, losses like

Dandridge v. Williams (394 U.S. 254 [1970]), *Wyman v. James* (400 U.S. 309 [1971]), and others (see Bussiere 1997, 155 n. 5) marked a decline in the vitality of the welfare rights movement. In combination with broader political and legal changes as well as increasing tensions within welfare rights organizations themselves, Bussiere argues, "the Court's adverse decisions crippled the welfare rights movement, which ultimately collapsed in 1975" (11). The experiences of the welfare rights movement show how powerful a combination activists, attorneys, responsive courts, and a mobilized constituency can be, at least for a time. Decisions in the era went beyond the straightforward enforcement of clearly existing rights to build new claims and understandings regarding the legal status of the poor. And, although the streams of correlation and causation are complex, it is worth noting that this period of pronounced legal activism largely overlaps with the short-lived declaration era in welfare—a time, we saw, when the poor were taken largely on their word when they presented their cases.

In contrast, the period of the 1990s seemed to lack everything that had marked the era of the welfare rights movement—except, of course, poverty and injustice. Legal service attorneys were hindered by new restrictions on both budgets and litigation, client organizations had dwindled, courts were in the hands of new and sharply conservative majorities. Political leaders were increasingly hostile to the poor and embraced new technologies of surveillance in widely touted battles against "fraud, waste, and abuse." In the pages that follow, we see a number of complaints about welfare surveillance. In different conditions, many of them could, theoretically, be translated into legal claims to, say, a right to privacy, a right against unreasonable searches, or a right against "consent" under conditions of duress (Reich 1963, 1965). But the point is that they aren't.[4]

Complaining about CRIS-E

This section centers on the interviews with three women—Jamaica, Jessie, and Moonstar—to explore the ways in which they talk about the surveillance capacities of the welfare bureaucracy. In the previous chapter, we looked at a series of longer excerpts with an interest in understanding the broader terms of the clients' relationships with the welfare bureaucracy; here, we focus more narrowly on the processes and politics of the surveillance programs.

Jamaica

Jamaica is the single mother of a four-year-old. She has been receiving assistance since her pregnancy. Jamaica and Cindy, the interviewer, are talking about the extensive documentation needed when one applied for benefits.

> C: How did you feel about the welfare offices wanting to know all that information?
>
> J: It's stupid.
>
> C: Why?
>
> J: Every time you go in there for a face-to-face interview they want it again and they already got it, got most of it.
>
> C: So you have to take it back each time for your reevaluation.
>
> J: Sure.
>
> C: Why do you think they want so much information about you?
>
> J: Because they are nosy.
>
> C: Tell me?
>
> J: Their nose itches . . . it's the government . . . you know, they want their nose in everything.
>
> C: Why do you think that is, what have you thought about it before, before we talked about it?
>
> J: Government. I feel the government is going toward communism, I really do.
>
> C: You do?
>
> J: Yes.
>
> C: They ask you for all this information, do you think that if you didn't give it to them, like if you had a job, and didn't tell them, do you think they could find out?
>
> J: Of course.
>
> C: How?
>
> J: All they have to do is run your Social Security number and they got you.
>
> [later]
>
> C: Do you know what kinds of information the computer has about you?

J: Everything. As far as I'm concerned they know everything except the last time you shit. I mean that is the truth.

C: Like what kinds of things?

J: They know your age, when you were born, your Social Security number, address, everything. . . . They know everything. What color hair you have, what color eyes you have. . . . You know, the only thing I don't think they know is what size pants I wear.

C: But you are not sure?

J: They might know that, too.

C: What else do you think they know?

J: They know everything, where I have worked, they know everything. . . .

C: Why do you think they want to know all this?

J: Because they are nosy. . . . They are really nosy. . . . They want their nose stuck up everybody's ass.

C: How you feel about them being so nosy?

J: It's none of their fucking business.

It would be hard to argue that Jamaica accepts the "legitimacy" of the surveillance regime with which she lives. She depicts the surveillance capacity of the state in sweeping terms, but then critiques it in very personal terms, as if they are just busybodies or snoops with a voyeuristic bent. As discussed below, one could argue that Jamaica's closing statement that "it's none of their fucking business" is the street version of the claim to a privacy right protecting her from illegitimate state intrusion. Her statement, like others' complaints that the state is nosy or butting in, serves the rights-like function of raising important questions about the limits on legitimate government intrusion. It also, probably, has the potential to develop into a more full-blown rights-based critique. But that is just the point here: these *potential* rights claims are so personal, so diverse, and—qua rights claims—so undeveloped. Jamaica and the others have not, to use Michael McCann's terms, "appropriated the language of rights to interpret, or 'name,' a long-experienced injustice" (1994, 89).

Jessie

Jessie is a twenty-one-year-old mother of one child. She and Karen, the interviewer, had just finished talking about the extensive documentation and verification procedures.

K: Why do you think they want to know all that stuff about you?

J: I don't know. I really don't.

K: Take a guess.

J: Just so they can be butting in more or less.

K: What do you mean by butting in?

J: They don't need to know my business and they have been [wanting to] here lately. They have been wanting every little detail.

K: Can you give me an example?

J: Why am I going back to school. Why don't I have a job. Who is babysitting my child. If I'm giving them money or anything.

K: How does that make you feel?

J: Just makes me feel like, I don't know, like . . . it just makes me feel strange that they know everything about me and I don't like that.

K: Can you explain more about "strange." What about this bothers you?

J: Because they just know everything about me and I don't like it because I'm only getting so much a month. . . . I'm a person that likes to keep to myself and if I had known all the stuff I had to go through to get on it I would not have done it again.

K: How does it make you feel?

J: I don't like being on welfare. I never did. I feel like I can't do as much as what I want to do. And my child, I can't provide for her more [of] what I want for her.

[later]

K: The welfare office is able to do what are called computer number matches, where they use the Social Security numbers of people in your family to look and see if you have money or income that you're not reporting. They use information from state and federal taxes, Social Security information, statewide wage records, and information from unemployment compensation, worker's comp., and state retirement systems. They make a computer check of this information several times a

year and your caseworker gets all of this information. Did you
know your worker gets this information?

J: No I did not.

K: How does that make you feel to know they are looking at you
like this?

J: They act like they own us.

K: How does that make you feel?

J: It makes me feel real low. There is no sense in it and they
shouldn't be butting in business where they shouldn't be.

K: Why do you think they do this?

J: To keep you from getting more. Like if you had a bank account
they keep you . . . from getting more [of] what you want.

K: How does that make you feel?

J: I feel that I can do better than being on welfare. I'm trying my
damnedest. I'll be getting off real soon.

Jessie's commentary replicates a pattern seen in many other interviews in which a discussion of specific problems or facets of a program continually returns to more general complaints about the way
they are treated and the difficulty of life on welfare—"they act like
they own you," "it makes me feel real low," "I'll be getting off real
soon."[5] Like Jamaica, who thought that the welfare agency should
mind their own business, Jessie's antisurveillance protest is a similarly
personal argument that it should quit butting in. Jessie is also like
many of us in that she seems to be unaware of the extent of surveillance around her. Although posters, caseworkers, and consent forms
all discuss the various measures taken, Jessie—along with millions of
other Americans who are oblivious to the various transaction analyses, communication trackings, and security measures in their lives—
says she just didn't know. If, as Gary Marx (1999) has argued, one
of the key demands of an ethical surveillance program is that the surveilled are fully aware of the system, then welfare surveillance falls
short of the mark.

Moonstar

Moonstar is the mother of two children. She has been receiving assistance for the twelve years since her employer, a major state institution, closed. Although she voices her complaints about privacy, no-

tice again how the privacy concern quickly ties into her overall frustration with welfare dependency.

> C: Why do they want [the information about your household and bills]?
>
> M: I really don't know. I think it's an invasion of privacy. I don't think that they need [it]. They only need certain things to determine how much money you should get. They don't need your whole life's back, past, and future, and present.
>
> C: Talk more about "invasion of privacy."
>
> M: Well, they want to know everything. I mean everything. How many people you got living with you and that's nobody's business. How much rent you pay. How much utilities you pay and if you can't pay it then that's tough luck. They put everything on this big screen and anybody and everybody can look right there on that big screen and say, "Oh look at this."
>
> C: Can anybody find out this information on you?
>
> M: I think they could, I think they really could.
>
> C: How does that make you feel . . . ?
>
> M: Well, I feel cheap when I walk in there. I feel that everybody's looking at me and like she ain't got no job, she's dirty, and I just feel worse when I go in there and come out than I did going there. I don't like asking for help but I had to. And I just don't like it and I should have got off it a long time ago because I don't like everybody knowing me too good.

Rights Talk

The complaints about welfare and welfare surveillance are multifaceted. We hear about the client's difficulty finding required numbers and forms, their frustration with rules that are effectively impossible to obey, their fear of an error or violation being discovered, their sense of degradation and disfranchisement by the bureaucracy, their offense at the snooping, and their sense that all of the hassles are a form of punishment for being poor. This diversity of claims probably typifies much everyday conversation about conflicts, challenges, and personally important politics. By the time stories of conflict get distilled into the professional forms that they take in the media, in the academy, or in the courtroom, much of the real messiness of everyday life has been edited away. In some important ways, removing that messiness is a significant step in political articulation and mobilization—individuals can unite with others, find common terms, and present a unified and focused critique. The language of rights has played a critical and ongoing role in these processes. But in other ways, the ongoing editing of American political discourse can work to exclude marginal perspectives and undercut creative analysis as our language calcifies around fixed terms and categories. This book began with the argument that we face such a calcification in our conversations about surveillance technology, and we now seek to explore the "messiness" of everyday conversations as part of a quest for new perspectives and ideas.

In the diversity that marks these conversations there are numerous arguments that sound like the language of privacy rights. Along with Mary, three others explicitly complained that the computer matching program violated their legal rights, ten made passing reference to their "privacy" or their "private business," thirteen used more personal language like saying that the welfare agency was nosy, ought to "mind its own business" or was "getting too personal." The complaint that one is "nosy" or should "mind their own business," is a vernacular claim to a right of privacy and could readily translate into a more formally legal grievance. We can easily picture an organizer or activist attorney translating all these claims into the more formal terms, like "the right to privacy," that have dominated mainstream conversations about surveillance. I suppose that I, as the author of this book, could declare that all of these claims are *"really"* assertions of the grand old right to privacy and should be read as such.

But such a move seems inappropriate because neither the language, the actions, nor the contexts surrounding these claims call for such a declaration. Noting these reticences on things like privacy and rights is not to argue that they are somehow completely "absent." As discussed in the beginning of this work, the language of privacy rights is the nation's leading framework for the deliberation and discussion of surveillance. It would thus be totally improbable to think that dozens of conversations about surveillance could avoid these terms. What occurs here is not a complete silence, but a quieting of the privacy rights framework as other issues and moral frameworks push to the forefront.

What is noteworthy here is that so few of the interviewees make the relatively short step that Mary made; from complaints about nosiness to statements about rights. (Fewer still—only two—have ever made a formal assertion of rights through the state's "Fair Hearing" process.) In sum, unlike the interviewees in *Rights at Work*, who "spontaneously invoked the language of rights" (McCann 1994, 235),[6] in this group it was the rare interview that would lead one to conclude that they were hearing that language. Even more rare is any sort of story indicating that a client took some sort of action to assert her rights.[7]

Rare, but not unheard of. The opening to this chapter shows how Mary seemed to pick up a more forceful language as she turned to language of rights—once she had said the word "rights," the word "Constitution" shortly followed, and, within a moment, she was calling for "protest." The story of one other woman also helps us to understand the ways in which law can be empowering.

Jessica

Here, Cindy interviews Jessica, a mother of three who has been on and off AFDC and the other programs for a decade. What begins as a dark comedy about a visibly pregnant woman being required to get a doctor's statement to prove that she is pregnant turns into an interesting tale about how the welfare computers know more about a couple's finances than they themselves, and about the apparently decisive power of a lawyer in the struggle that ensues. Cindy has just asked Jessica how she felt about the forms and paperwork she faced when she first applied for welfare:

> J: Truthfully I didn't mind. I didn't mind bringing in the papers. What upset me was when I was pregnant and the lady could see that I was pregnant. I mean that I was sticking way out [and] she looked at me like I was lying. Like I wasn't pregnant and I was just making it up. I was upset about that. But I can understand why they need documentation because there's a lot of people who try to fraud. And I can understand why they wanted it, but it upset me that when I was in dire need of it

and we didn't have any other income and she looked at me like I was lying.

C: So what did you have to do to prove that you were pregnant?

J: Go get another pregnancy statement from the doctor.

C: Why do you think they ask for so much information?

J: Because they are nosy. I think they want to know everything. They already know everything about you if you are on the computer. They know everything about you. It is either to give themselves more work to do or to give you the run-around. I don't know. I guess I can understand it, why they have it, if they are afraid that people is going to fraud them and they want to make sure that you really don't have anything. You know when you tell them you don't have anything, they want to make sure you don't have anything.

C: Do you think they would find out if you took a job in another county and didn't report?

J: Oh yeah. I think they could find out. As long as you are receiving a pay stub I think they could find out. Because your name is going through somebody's computer somewhere and they are making you out a check and you are cashing that check at a bank, I think they could find out. As a matter of fact, I know they could find out. I know people that has had that done to them.

C: That was working and didn't report?

J: Oh yeah. That got caught and went to jail.

C: . . . how about saving in a bank in another state and you didn't report?

J: Yes, I think they could find all that about you.

C: How?

J: Because I think they have all of us in a computer and when they know, if they know we are working, or they suspect it they go through and check all these, I don't know how they do it, but they check all these by a list and they check all these places. And I think if you had money in a bank and you was receiving a bank statement it would be easy for them find out.

You might be able to get away with it for a while. But I know that we had at one time had received some workmen's comp checks that got lost in the mail and we did not know that we had these checks and we were living [elsewhere] and we did not know we was getting them. We was already in

[this] county like a year later. We didn't even know that we
had the checks up there or I'd have been up there getting
them. We didn't know or I would have notified the welfare
and all that. But because we didn't know that we had them
we just went on with our life and she called and the lady had
called us up at home and told us that we was frauding the welfare department and my husband had to go up there and have
a big old argument with these people in order for them to realize. Our lawyer had to be involved and everything before
they realized that we did not know that we had these checks.

C: You went to the welfare office?

J: Oh yeah, they was going to put us in jail.

C: And you didn't know you were getting these?

J: We didn't know we had them. They were lost in the mail and
they were up at the post office [where we used to live] and we
didn't know we had the checks. The welfare called us and said
that we had all this money that we didn't report and I told
them that we didn't know that we had all this money. If we
would have known we would have told them. . . .

   We called his lawyer [who had helped with the worker's
compensation case] and [he] put a trace on the checks and
found out that is where the checks were at and the welfare
didn't want to believe us. The lawyer had to contact them and
tell them that we did not know that we had these checks. They
had never been cashed or anything.

C: How do you think they found out about those checks?

J: Because I think we are all in a big computer and they find out
everything about us.

C: Was this your lawyer?

J: It was my husband's lawyer

C: [surprised] [He had] his own lawyer to do that?

J: Yeah. He was nice enough to call and do it for us. I thought he
was going to go to jail over it. I mean we had a big fight with
them. We had to go up there and they treated us like dirt. And
we didn't even know. I think that the amount of money was
that they was fighting over us was about $1,000 or less. . . .
they were going to put us in jail over it.

C: Your lawyer went to the welfare office?

J: He called . . . them. . . . I think that he probably did a little bit
of good in calling them.

Clearly, things like rights and lawyers can be important allies in these struggles, whether it is to give voice to frustrations of someone like Mary or to make a few phone calls which help to keep Jessica out of jail. In broader terms, as we have seen, the welfare rights movement of the 1960s was able to bring about important victories for the welfare poor through a combination of scholarship, lawyering, and protest. In the late 1970s, too, court challenges by advocates of the poor were able to bring about some due process improvements in the administration of the early computer matching programs.[8]

The Context of Consciousness

Since the language of rights can be so helpful, has been important in past struggles by the poor, and, more generally, is such a core element of American political discourse (see Glendon 1991; Scheingold 1974; Tocqueville 1969 [1835]), it may seem surprising to find some Americans who do not voice their grievances about government intrusions in the form of rights claims. But empirical studies have suggested that the turn to rights talk is neither so very widespread nor entirely automatic (Bumiller 1988; Merry 1990; Engel and Munger 1996). Rather, the turn to rights requires a social context or setting in which there is some real sense of efficacy and hope, as well as a subject or citizen who finds some meaning and benefit in the vocabulary. As McCann argues in *Rights at Work* (1994), his study of the women's pay equity movement, the long-felt injustices surrounding gender-based salary discrimination were only translated into "the language of rights" and legal mobilization after there was some sign of institutional support.[9]

McCann explains that the rights claims of pay equity activists emerged in a context shaped by women's experiences in the workplace and labor unions as well as by the legacy of legal empowerment won in the women's rights movement and formalized in affirmative action policies. Further, he notes, activist attorneys pursued publicity campaigns intended to instigate and bolster rights-based consciousness among women workers. He also notes that the mobilization of rights could only be sustained in conditions of relatively high solidarity, organizational support, and effective leadership (1994, 92–137): "We thus again emphasize that pay equity rights claims arose not out of thin air, but rather within a context of opportunities and expectations prefigured by the terms of evolving political struggles over state-authorized legal rights" (1994, 104; see also Zemans 1983, 695).

A similar point regarding the importance of context and condition in the formation and mobilization of rights claims and protest was made by Piven and Cloward in *Poor People's Movements:*

> The occasions when protest is possible among the poor, the forms that it must take, and the impact that it can have are all delimited by the social structure in ways that usually diminish its extent and diminish its force. . . . The emergence of a protest movement entails a transformation both of consciousness and of behavior. The change in consciousness has at least three distinct aspects. First, "the system"—or those aspects of the system that people experience and perceive—loses legitimacy. Large numbers of men and women who ordinarily accept the authority of their rulers and the legitimacy of institutional arrangements come to believe in some measure that these rulers and the arrangements are unjust and wrong. Second, *people who are ordinarily fatalistic, who believe that existing arrangements are inevitable, begin to assert "rights" that imply demands for change.* Third, there is a new sense of efficacy; people who ordinarily consider themselves helpless come to believe that they have some capacity to change their lot. (1979, 3–4, emphasis added)

What the research here suggests is that the potential assertion of "rights that imply demands for change" has simply not occurred, despite conditions and sentiments that seem to call forth such an assertion. Using Piven and Cloward's terms, there is little evidence to suggest that more than a few women in this sample "accept the authority of their rulers and the legitimacy of institutional arrangements." Like the welfare poor interviewed by Sarat (1990), there is little purchase for the idea that welfare administration is a legitimate, rule-bound system in which caseworkers and administrators fairly and competently serve their clients.[10] These women complain about a broad range of the case management policies of the welfare agency—from obfuscation, to intimidating letters, to the number matches, to personal conflicts with caseworkers, to the constant suspicion and demands for verification which they must endure.

But, though the arrangements and rulers are seen as unjust, what we see here is that there is only a rare turn to the assertion of rights and no sign of the mobilization and empowerment which might follow. Surely, there are myriad factors involved in understanding how so many unique individuals come to such a place. We would want to look at, among other things, the absence of institutional conditions which would make rights talk more available, such as an active welfare rights movement, favorable court decisions, or visible legal activism. All of these things have been important parts of legal mobilization and should not be forgotten in the account which follows (McCann 1994; Scheingold 1974). But the important contribution that the research presented here can make is with an exploration of the everyday consciousness of people who are struggling with political domination on their own and in the absence of organization or support.

UNDERSTANDING RIGHTS RETICENCE: IGNORANCE, FEAR, NEED

For most of the clientele of these agencies [procedural rights] are irrelevant. . . . Welfare applicants and recipients are unaware of their entitlements and their procedural remedy, or they are fearful of challenging the welfare department, or they lack access to lawyers, advocates, or other resources with which to pursue their appeals.

Handler 1973, 147

What we see here is a group of people so uninformed about the basic rules and procedures, so frightened of getting in trouble with welfare regulations, and so needy and dependant upon welfare, that it seems hardly surprising that they feel, as did Mary, "that you give up your rights when you go on welfare."[11] The next few pages illustrate these three conditions.

Ignorance

Any time I have asked for a specific regulation or specific information or exactly what the rules are, or how much you are allowed for this or how much you are allowed, everyone is vague. No

one will tell you what the boundaries are until you have crossed
them. . . . I was patronized . . . and got no real information and I
let [my caseworker] do it. And I realized that she was doing it but
I didn't have the factual information to call her on it so I let it go.
[Question: Why do you think she didn't tell you?] Because it is
one of those things that if I have the information I can know if
I'm screwed. I know I can better take care of myself. I can know
the limits. I can know the boundaries.

Madeleine, mother of one

There is an institutionally constructed and pervasive lack of information and knowledge about the rules and procedures of the welfare
system. Many of the interviewees considered for this book had never
heard of some of the surveillance mechanisms that were in place.
Others did not know about the state's guarantee of a fair hearing
or about legal aid. Most did not know basic regulations dealing with
how much money could be made before it would affect benefit levels.
Others told us that when they had asked about this, they could get no
definite information. One woman told us how she received a vague
letter telling her to come in for an unexpected recertification hearing
—she spent the time waiting in horrible anxiety. Had someone made
a phone call about her? Had she violated some regulation that she
didn't know about? Would she lose her check, her food stamps, and
her medical card?

Another wanted to know how much monthly income she could
earn through a potential part-time job before she would affect her
food stamps and her medical card. The caseworker's response was, we
really can't say, just do the best you can, and we'll figure it out later.
Of course, she could not take the job because of the unknown risk to
her crucial support and health care. Disempowered by what seems
to be a situation of intentional information withholding by the welfare department (or in some cases, welfare workers explain, rules are
so complex and subject to diverse interpretation that the caseworkers
simply cannot explain the hypothetical outcome of a change in status;
see also Sarat 1990, 345 n. 5), these women lack a very basic knowledge of the complex system that would be required to make any procedural or legal challenge to its administration. It is an ironic revela-

tion of the imbalance of power at work here: the welfare bureaucracy which demands total disclosure from its clients cloaks itself in the secrecy of massive obfuscation.

Fear

My caseworker one time lost some papers, some copies of some paycheck stubs, and called me and told me that I was gonna get it. That if they came out from Columbus and pulled my file that I would be arrested for welfare fraud and that I would go to prison and I was pregnant for my daughter at the time. And, see, it was her mistake, where she had lost the copies that I had gave her and she tried to blame it on me. And I had to take them all back up there again because I had my receipt showing where I had brought them in and got them copied at the front desk. And I mean you know it is just scary. It's scary, and if you are not worried about not being able to feed your children or have a home to sleep in, you are worried about whether you are going to go to prison for welfare fraud. They make it hard any way you go.

Eleanor, a mother of two who has been on AFDC for eight years

These women fear that their caseworkers will sanction them if they complain. They fear that a neighbor or angry relative will make a "rat call" to inform the Department of Human Services about a part-time job or a live-in boyfriend. They fear "rocking the boat," "making waves," "stirring up shit," or any other thing that might call attention to themselves, because of their expectation that it would only lead to a close inspection and potential reclassification of their case. In short, they fear that complaining might start a process that would get out of their control (Bumiller 1987, 436). Most of all, they fear that something will happen which would cause them to lose their check and their medical card and cross the thin line to homelessness.

It is important to recognize how vulnerable these women are as they deal with both the welfare office and the people in their broader communities. Because AFDC benefits are set well below a livable budget, some forms of extra income are virtually necessitated (Mary received $421 per month for a family of four and $350 went to her landlord; see Edin 1993).[12] As Moonstar explains:

> The only way that you can make it, if you make it, is by working under the table. . . . Welfare don't give you enough money to barely make it and you have to do little things just to keep your head afloat. . . . I have no money in the end because I pay all the money. I have no money at the end. And the ADC is supposed to be for dependent children. How can I take care of my kids when I have got to pay everything in the household and not have no money to take care of my children? . . . I have to go out and make a little extra money because I don't get enough to support my family, pay the bills, and be able to buy my kids shoes. If I have to go out and mow a yard for $10 that will get my kids extra shoes. Because my bills takes all of my money, every bit of it.

The simple fact that "welfare recipients cannot live on their benefits alone" (Edin 1993, 37) requires them to break some of the rules and regulations in order to earn or hide some extra form of income or support. They do this because they must, and because they do it, they live in fear of jail time, financial penalties, and loss of benefits. Their situation and their fear put them in a weakened position as they deal with the welfare office or their caseworkers. Many said they didn't want to "rock the boat" or make a lot of trouble which would bring their "whole case in for inspection."[13] And one woman explained the low use of "Fair Hearings" this way:

> [People are] afraid they are going to go in and inspect everything in their life. See what they have and what they don't have. You know a lot of people go in and say they only have one car or have more or something like that. Just things like that. It would be like an audit type thing to them. You know, "if you cause trouble then we are going to do this to you" and stuff like that. And give them more grief. They'll make them do more paper work and they are real good about that.

The fear of retribution keeps most from raising any protest with the agency, but it is also important to recognize how the fear and disempowerment is even more pervasive than the fear of retribution from the welfare agency alone. As noted, in these small towns, the welfare department actively encourages citizens to make "rat calls" to turn in "cheaters." Balloons, pencils, flyswatters, even mouse pads and beverage can insulators, with inscriptions like "Welfare Fraud Is Wrong!" or "Report Welfare Fraud!" are distributed at fairs and displayed in offices and waiting rooms at the Department of Human Services. So, as these women deal with ex-spouses and relatives, neighbors, landlords, shopkeepers, and others in their community, they are in a situation that could only be described as perpetual potential blackmail. Anyone who knows that they receive welfare benefits holds the power to do great damage or, at least, create major hassles in these women's lives. In this way, the net of state surveillance goes beyond the already able reach of the computers and caseworkers, permeating local communities with watchful eyes.

Need

You have to go along with the system, like I said, in order to get a check. . . . You are just a poor person that absolutely needs welfare and, yeah, you lose your rights when you go on assistance.

Mary

I had to apply for the welfare because my now ex-husband left with all of our money. He left me owing a lot of bills. Soon after he left, my father passed away. I was evicted from my home because [my husband] took all the money to go back to his home. We lived in an unheated, unfinished garage. We had no running water. No toilets. No bathrooms. We used a port-a-pot and we used to carry water. I cooked on a small wooden heating stove and we had cement floors. Snow sifted through the ceilings when it was snowing and I knew I had to do something to get out of there.

Linda, mother of two children, aged two and eight

In many senses, hard times define the rural counties of Appalachian Ohio. Coal mining, historically a primary source of employment, is far less labor-intensive than it once was. Industry is declining. Education levels are low. Roughly a quarter of the population lives below the poverty line and many more struggle just above it. Child care is hard to come by, full-time jobs harder still, and most jobs for unskilled people pay low wages and do not provide medical insurance. By turning to the Department of Human Services, the women can get a supply of food, a check to cover the rent but not much else (a lucky few might get housing assistance), and they get what often seems most important to these parents, Medicaid coverage for their families. This situation of desperate need and few if any alternatives to welfare augments the powerlessness of the Appalachian poor. With no other realistic alternatives to their welfare status, they must readily accept the terms of the system, the edicts of the caseworkers, and the regulations, limitations, and enforcement mechanisms that come with it.

THE RIGHTSLESS

These are frightened, often lonely, women and children who live on the edge of hunger and homelessness and in fear of their caseworkers and their neighbors. They are, for the most part, isolated from each other and unwilling or unable to talk with others about their experiences on welfare, their coping mechanisms, or their shared plight. They are in Appalachian small towns and rural areas that lack the economic vitality of other regions. They live in a time when the poor are vilified by local and national political leaders. They lack a knowledge of the system of rules and procedures that engulfs them, and a remarkable number of them are unaware of basic guarantees like Fair Hearings or legal counsel.[14] They lack effective political or legal representation and they even lack the formal legal position that might lead to a mobilization of rights. Without the knowledge, the forum, or the resources to wage any sort of battles about what bothers them, they are stuck in a cycle of powerlessness.[15]

Other groups have experienced some, if limited, success in making and mobilizing legal claims over grievances. McCann's *Rights at Work* details the mobilization of law and the concomitant empowerment of women workers in the pay equity movement of the 1980s: "[P]ay equity activism has both reflected and deepened the growing legal rights consciousness among women workers in the United States. Not only have many working women been mobilized for action around specific new rights claims, but these activists have become increasingly involved and sophisticated in mobilizing rights as a political resource generally. This transformative process has been

evident in interviewees' critical understandings about legally constituted power relations, their increased sense of entitlement to fair
treatment, and their testimony about new solidaristic bonds and other
resources that the movement has generated to challenge unjust workplace relations" (McCann 1994, 276).

In the study at hand, as we look at *potential* rights consciousness
and mobilization among the Appalachian welfare poor, we see what
is really the inverse of the process identified in McCann's work. The
legal mobilization that took place around pay equity issues occurred
because women felt that they had been wronged *and* because they had
the social, legal, economic, and political resources to do something
about it: the 1964 Civil Rights Act; a union movement; activist attorneys; financial resources. The women interviewed here—disentitled,
uninformed, scared, alone, and dependent—missed the "growing legal rights consciousness," have not "mobilized for action," have not
created "specific new rights claims," and have not become "increasingly involved and sophisticated." Instead, they have grumbled and
avoided trouble, while turning to quiet personal strategies of resistance through which they find ways to get a little extra money
each month. It is as if the escalation and empowerment identified in
McCann's project work in the reverse—few economic or political resources, little education, little solidarity, no organizational structure,
no hope of putting rights to work. The sense of rights felt by the
unionized and mobilized women involved in the pay equity movement is in sharp contrast to the experience of the welfare poor.

Welfare mothers, as constituted by their ongoing relationships
and status within the welfare bureaucracy, are almost the inverse of
the rights-bearing individual who would rise up against surveillance
with a legal challenge.[16] Given the structural, institutional, and social
pressures that push against an assertion of rights in this setting, it is
not at all surprising that we see such silence surrounding these potentially empowering terms of the legal system—indeed, what is perhaps surprising is that there are even a few people in this group who
do use such claims.

Conclusion

> To know the uses of law, we need to know not only how and by
> whom the law is used, but also when and by whom it is not.
>
> *Ewick and Silbey 1992, 737*

There are significant pressures and tendencies against rights-claiming in the everyday lives of these welfare mothers. In other times, places, or conditions, these tendencies might be different, but here they are not. One is almost forced to share Nancy Fraser's sad conclusion that welfare mothers are a class of people that "largely lacks rights" (1989, 154). The rights reticence of this population both signifies and advances a cycle of disempowerment which has been widely identified among the welfare poor, even as it demonstrates their disconnection from a language and framework which may have the potential for significant political leverage.

Questions about the nature and magnitude of the empowerment that a rights approach might bring, what costs would be associated with it, and how it might make sense of the issues at hand for the people at hand have been thoroughly discussed in the literature on the politics of rights (Kiss 1997; Silverstein 1996; McCann 1994; Rosenberg 1991; Minow 1990; Williams 1987; Schneider 1986; Scheingold 1974).

What we turn to here is a closer look at what these women say in lieu of rights talk. It seems clear that their legal consciousness is one of entrapment, fear, and some mystification, rather than the sort of empowering ascension to rights we might see elsewhere.[17] But there are, of course, other ways of thinking besides *the law*—other languages and sensibilities which can express unique critical perspectives, explain personal choices, and shed new light on the limits of law's vocabulary.[18] As argued in the next chapter, many of these women deploy an alternative to the discourse of rights and justice—a more personalized discourse of need, care, and responsibility. And they follow an alternative to legal or political mobilization with daily actions seeking to frustrate the mission of the welfare bureaucracy and its surveillance system.

CHAPTER FOUR

The Need to Resist

If you have kids, you will do anything for your kids. I mean, I do.
So it's not really illegal.

Coco, a mother of one

WITH THE EXCEPTION OF one or two people, no one here says,
"I am an American citizen, and this cannot be done to me." No
one says, "This is a violation of my privacy rights and an immolation
of the spirit of the Fourth Amendment." But most of them do find
ways to speak *and* act out their opposition to the surveillance regime.
What do they say? And what do they do?

●

Dewey, a single mother of four, talks to Cindy:

> D: When it comes between you and your family and a computer,
> there's always a way to do it.
> C: So you think the computer system is probably not going to
> stop people from getting extra money to make it through the
> month?
> D: If they are like me, your kids come first. And if I need some-
> thing to get through the end of the month with them, I will
> do it.

●

Shawana, a married mother of three, talks with Karen:

> K: How do you feel about, in general, not reporting, in reference
> to yourself or in reference to other people who don't report

income, bank accounts, assets that technically they are supposed to report?

S: Well, that makes you feel, well, yeah, like you are ripping
them off. Like you are a thief.

K: Do you feel that your babysitting that you didn't report—
and your bank accounts—do you feel that you are ripping
them off?

S: Yeah, to an extent. I try to live honestly and that is sort of a
contradiction, a contradiction to myself, but I'm not willing
to tell them the truth about that.

K: How do you feel about it being a contradiction, how uncomfortable are you with it?

S: Well, fairly uncomfortable. You know I don't think about it
very often, but talking about it makes me feel pretty bad.

K: Do you see any need to do anything differently?

S: No.

K: Can you tell me why? You have said that it makes you feel uncomfortable now that we are talking about it, but you don't feel
any need to do anything differently. Can you explain . . . why?

S: For my survival.

•

Delilah and Cindy discuss the same topics:

C: You said that sometimes you cut hair, and sometimes you help
your brother wallpaper. And you know all these other people
who have to do something to make ends meet when they are
on ADC. How do you feel about that?

D: I think as long as someone is using what they are doing for
their home or they are buying something that their kids need,
I don't see anything wrong with it. If they are going out and
they are doing it and they are boozing it up and they are using
drugs, I think that's a shame. . . . [For] me it always went to my
daughter. It always went into the house or into my car or my
gas tank or maybe for something that Kelly needs that she
would not have otherwise.

C: Do you think most of the people are like yourself?

D: I think they are doing it, most, the majority are doing it to
better their home and their family.

•

Elizabeth and Cindy:

C: Have you ever had to keep the truth from the welfare office about something?

E: No.

C: About your family or income?

E: I stay with my mom right now and I don't help her as much as they think I do but every little bit helps her and then it helps me too. That's the only thing. You can get ahead. You bend it a little bit.

C: You mean like you tell them that you have to give her more money than you really give her.

E: Yeah.

C: You never got caught doing that?

E: Not yet. Things happen.

C: Do you worry about it?

E: A little, but my girl means more to me than what they're gonna do.

Lisa and Roxy get financial gifts from their parents. Amy babysits on the side and keeps the money in a locked box in her house. She explains: "You realize that there are things that they don't need to know." The poor fight budget-busting limits on income and resources by engaging in a widespread cash economy and hustling whatever money and help they can. According to the interviews undertaken here as well as those in other studies, raising a family on welfare necessitates that a mother come up with some form of extra income. The simple facts that "welfare recipients cannot live on their benefits alone" (Edin 1993, 37), and that welfare agencies try to make sure that they do live on their benefits alone, set up a mean struggle between clients and the agencies.

Strip away the bureaucratic language of fraud control, regulatory enforcement, consent forms, and the like, and we see a simple pattern in which a government agency is using broadly targeted and ongoing surveillance in an effort to force a dependent population to live at an intolerable level of poverty. As the Department of Human Services uses its surveillance system in an attempt to deter or punish behavior which their clients define as both necessary and moral, an ongoing pattern of domination and resistance ensues. As the mothers resist, it will be argued below, they not only resist the specific commands of the state welfare policy, but the related demand that the books of their lives be open to total surveillance. And as they take these actions, they build a reality of personal identity that challenges the debilitating depictions of the state and the society—the asserted portrait of the poor, lazy, neglectful parent is challenged by a necessarily secret life of smarts, of work, and of being a good mother.

In the quotations from women like Dewey, Shawana, Delilah, and Elizabeth, this pattern of everyday struggle with the welfare bureaucracy and its surveillance system is explained in terms that come out of their situations of poverty and parenthood—they focus on *need* and on their duties to *care for their families*. Their critique of welfare surveillance is one that we rarely hear in ongoing discussions of surveillance policy. What replaces, struggles with, or, in a few cases, complements talk about privacy rights as a form of critique and explanation is a critical ideology rooted in the everyday lives of the welfare mothers—one that turns on poverty, need, and children. Activities that produced extra income or support for their children were necessary and the surveillance mechanisms of the welfare department were criticized for making it more difficult to survive. The moral and critical framework advanced by these women reflects and makes sense of their daily experiences and demands. In very real and direct terms, it confronts the oppression and cruelty at work in our advanced systems of welfare surveillance. In so explicitly testifying to the power and impact of surveillance, their critique can strengthen and redefine our understanding of surveillance.

THE REVOLT OF THE GUARDS?

Although there are a lot of secrets to be kept in the struggle, it would be a mistake to conclude that the mothers' actions go unnoticed. Sociologists, caseworkers, human services directors, fraud control agents, political leaders—everyone involved in the politics of welfare knows that these practices occur. Some call it fraud or crime, others call it common sense. Some lambaste the poor as shiftless and immoral, others recognize that lower-income parents have a lot of needs to meet. Some deploy computer matches and investigators, others, as we see here, extend a bit of help.[1]

Interviews with welfare caseworkers and administrators in the region found that many of the frontline workers expressed profound sympathy for the plight of their clients. And we found that they, too, have forms of resistance through which they trick or evade the computer to meet the needs of clients that they would like to help. As noted in chapter 1, the welfare surveillance system is as much an effort to watch and control the caseworkers as it is to control the clients—the caseworkers know this and it frustrates them. As one put it:

> We're the caseworkers. We're the ones that can make a decision on something like this. There can be extenuating circumstances where we need to go in and make a change but we can't do it. They took all that away from us.
>
> The bottom line is that we work with common people, we work with sometimes ignorant people and we ought to have some control over what we do and they've taken all that control away from us.

This statement reveals the caseworkers' recognition of an explicit power struggle with their computerized system of control and clear resentment over their loss of autonomy. What we found in talking to caseworkers about their struggle with the system is that despite the obvious loss of a good deal of power, they still find small ways to take at least some of the control back. One simple example of this is seen in the case of food stamp coaching. In the calculation of food stamps, one important piece of information is whether a person prepares their food alone or with other people in their family or household. Normally, if a person prepares their food alone, the food stamp benefit will be higher than it would be if the individual is part of a food preparation group. Thus if four people share a house and receive food stamps, the household will get more stamps if they each prepare their food separately than if they prepare their meals together.

Of course, it is less important who is actually in the kitchen and at the table, then who the Department of Human Services believes is in the kitchen and at the table. So an applicant's statement regarding the nature of food purchasing, preparation, and consumption can have an important impact on their level of assistance. Based on interviews with caseworkers, it seems to be relatively common practice for caseworkers to avoid asking "How do you prepare and serve your food?"

but to ask "You don't prepare and eat your food together do you?" (often shaking head with a silent cue of "no"). In this way, the caseworker overrides the dictates of the system by communicating a little bit of insider information to an applicant. (Of course, applicants with system-savvy friends don't need the help because they can get pre-application advice which will be very likely to include this information regarding food stamp cases.)

In other times, the resistance is more overt and direct—frontally battling the computer system and its regulations with misinformation. In the first interview below, a caseworker (T) who came on after CRIS-E was in place tells the author (J) that she believes the system has been misprogrammed regarding some regulations. She explains her actions and decisions as well as the frustration over CRIS-E's almost dictatorial presence.

> T: It says you must do it this way and you'll do it that way and it will say no, it can't accept that. You can't argue with it and that's it. It's like this other person you've got in the room with us. And so you lie. And we don't know if we'll get in trouble for that or not.
>
> J: What do you do?
>
> T: Change ages. Change school attendance codes. Change work programs. Change disability. To get things to work. Household relationships; we change a lot of those.
>
> J: So you set up your own individual way of solving problems?
>
> T: I do it any way I can. . . . You have to [circumvent the system] to be able to do your job.
>
> J: Why?
>
> T: Because if the computer will just not group something, we can't just not give them benefits. That won't work. We can't wait until the state decides to reprogram it. I mean, we have to get these people a check if they're eligible for it and I guess you have to do it by whatever means possible because we have no other way. If you don't get a check from CRIS-E, we can't order you one, so yeah, you have to lie. And we've gotten very creative at it.

In a system which demands truth, goes to great lengths to verify truth, and heavily sanctions mistruth, this caseworker lies, even though "we don't know if we'll get in trouble for that or not." She does so, she says, because "we have to get these people their checks." Again, as with the clients, there are few signs or acts of frontal opposition from people who are busy, overworked, afraid of risking their job or seniority, and, importantly, without a claim that would be formally recognized in the system. How, after all, can a low-grade bureaucrat in a rural department of human services change the United States government's food stamp allocation system? In traditional understandings of politics, the odds look pretty sure that they simply can't. In this way they are just like the welfare mothers who have slim hope of bringing the state of Ohio to recalibrate its regulations to create a system which more effectively and fairly recognizes the medical and fiscal needs of young families. In the face of these long odds and low resources, we have seen that other, more quiet, tactics emerge. To recognize these tactics and assess their impact is not to argue that they are somehow a more effective or better form of politics than the more frontal, organized, and public confrontations undertaken by the poor in other times. And it is, surely, not to argue that a massive, widespread campaign for full rights to privacy, decent housing, and a livable income would not be a laudable idea. It is not necessary to see everyday resistance as a substitute for organized politics to recognize its existence, its importance, and its impact on the lives of these people.

THE POLITICS OF EVERYDAY RESISTANCE

Studies of resistance among peasant, poor, and working-class populations have identified and, in many cases, celebrated individual acts of defiance and evasion like that of the welfare mothers and caseworkers studied here.[2] They are what Scott called the "everyday forms" of resistance: "the ordinary weapons of relatively powerless groups: foot dragging, dissimulation, false compliance, pilfering, feigned ignorance, slander, arson, sabotage, and so forth." He explains, "When a peasant hides part of his crop to avoid paying taxes, he is both filling his stomach and depriving the state of gain. . . . When such acts are rare and isolated, they are of little interest; but when they become a consistent pattern (even though uncoordinated, let alone organized) we are dealing with resistance. The intrinsic nature and, in one sense, the 'beauty' of much peasant resistance is that it often confers immediate and concrete advantages, while at the same time denying resources to the appropriating classes, *and* that it requires little or no manifest organization" (1985, 29, 295–296).[3]

In thinking about the concept of "everyday resistance" it may be helpful to stress the *everyday* more than the *resistance*. That is, we speak here of practices and patterns of activity that may not be recognizable as traditional political action, may not have an interest in affecting or participating in public agendas, and may not even target specific political goals. The survival strategies of the welfare mothers were not, of course, invented or designed to thwart welfare surveillance. The things that they do—cut hair, sell things, adjust family units—have been done by poor people for centuries; they are simple actions of economic survival that have a long-standing history in rural and urban poverty (Halperin 1990; Stack 1974; Caudill 1963). As state welfare programs became available, it was an obvious move for the rural poor to include these new sources of money and support in their portfolios. But the state aid, bizarrely, came with strings attached: cease your long-standing survival patterns and entrepreneurial activity to become solely dependent on welfare. Generations-old patterns of survival were outlawed, illegalized by the new policies. Increasingly elaborate systems of surveillance and enforcement were erected in the effort to catch the poor doing what they had always done. "Getting by" was, to the state's way of seeing, now "welfare fraud" and the poor of the region became outlaw poachers (see also Thompson 1975).

When the poor continue their poaching in the face of a massive governmental effort to detect and stop them, they are rejecting and challenging, often by evasion, the political commands of the state. Although the mothers focus their attention on survival, not "politics," they clearly offer significant symbolic and material opposition to policy mandates. Activities such as this are not on the list of things that many would define as normal politics—voting, petitions, meetings, letters, and campaigns. But everyday practices of resistance are the sorts of politics that busy, threatened, and otherwise disempowered groups can, and do, use. And they are a type of politics that will be-

come far more important as state policies turn increasingly to regulation, surveillance, and meticulous enforcement. Once elaborate systems of bureaucratic surveillance are erected, it may be especially difficult to confront them with conventional political challenge. And as
mechanisms of surveillance push the issues of visibility and verification to the forefront of long-standing struggles between citizens and
institutions, practices of deception, camouflage, and secrecy are the
necessary politics of our times. *Everyday tactics of evasion, subterfuge,
and concealment, then, may very well become a defining form of politics in
the surveillance society.*

In the realm of conventional politics, many of the laws that seek
to improve the administration of data and surveillance programs include the requirement that the subjects of surveillance be allowed to
see and challenge records and conclusions regarding their lives. Because such laws make the largely erroneous assumption that many
people can or will take the time and initiative to review and challenge
mobile and constantly changing information files that they may not
even be aware of, these laws are, while necessary, a wildly inadequate
measure for the control of surveillance regimes. What is far more important is to work toward ensuring the full participation of affected
publics in the very basic processes of setting the goals, premises, and
designs of the systems themselves. But this is a remarkable, if not
insurmountable, challenge, since large-scale systems of surveillance
have their origins and design in the exclusive and technocratic realms
of law enforcement, corporate management, and government bureaucracy. It is, in many ways, these barriers confronting the idea of
effective popular participation in the formal design and implementation of surveillance and information systems that draws so much
of our attention to the issue of everyday resistance—a form of participation on the part of people whose voices and values are excluded
from the design and implementation of surveillance programs that
will have such an immense impact on their lives.

At this point, we should pause and consider just how widespread
the patterns of everyday resistance to surveillance programs are.
When employee drug-testing programs came on line in the mid-
1980s, small companies emerged selling "clean urine" in magazines

and newspapers. When police begin using radar to detect speeders, drivers begin installing radar detectors. In the United Kingdom, recent installations of closed-circuit television cameras in public parks and business districts pushed antisurveillance activists to destroy or damage cameras, and, additionally, to undertake creative campaigns involving, among other things, signal jamming, faked emergencies, and the use of mirrors to disarm the surveillance systems (see Davies 1999, 254–256). Simon Davies notes that the 1970s anti-census "protest in the Netherlands was so widespread that it achieved a critical mass that finally made the census entirely unworkable. A substantial number of Dutch citizens simply refused to supply information to the census authority" (1999, 245). Here, in the United States, when the Internal Revenue Service develops profiles which it uses to identify those who are to be audited, tax advisors, newspapers, and Web sites broadcast the parameters of those profiles in a very public manner. Herds of tax attorneys and preparers assist middle-class and wealthy families as well as businesses in shirking, as much as possible, the obligations of taxation and besting the surveillance systems designed to enforce the fulfilling of those obligations. Really, in these ongoing battles to prepare and divide the pie of national finance, the welfare mothers do nothing different from what many typical families would do, and they do it from a position of greater need and risk and with less advice and support. It may be, then, that these high-tech versions of the welfare mothers' tricks will come into wide use as more and more of the general public meets the scrutiny that the poor have known for so long. Indeed, recent reports suggest that one of the most vital new areas of invention and growth in the computer industry is concerned with providing sophisticated new tools for encrypting, anonymizing, and hiding (Lester 2001).

When viewed from this perspective, there are millions upon millions of people throughout the world engaged in widespread and diverse types of opposition and resistance to surveillance regimes. Depending on class, context, and circumstance, some get more formal, public, and organized, while others must necessarily remain personal, private, and alone. Some types of resisters—like the upper-middle-class tax shirker—are tolerated, even smiled upon, by political leaders. Others, like the poor women here, are vilified and hunted. In all these different contexts and manners, the politics of surveillance are played out on a daily basis. It is here, rather than in the official arenas of the courts, legislatures, and blue-ribbon commissions, that the most important and dynamic politics of surveillance may be taking place.

These recognitions and possibilities mean that we should take particular interest in how practices of everyday resistance work as forms of politics. There is a danger, it has been noted, that depicting something like petty fraud as a vital form of politics may well give false amplification to insignificant gestures, place false hope in tiny acts of individual defiance, and give inappropriate, if implicit, approval to what are often selfish and destructive acts (see Handler 1992, McCann and March 1995).[4] A full examination of everyday resistance as a form of political struggle calls forth further questions about the nature, impact, and ideology of resistant practices. Do acts of everyday resistance produce any tangible improvements in the lot of the resister and, even, others? Are acts of everyday resistance purely the isolated tactics of self-interested, even antisocial, individuals? Is there any sort of sharing or collaboration which could be laying the groundwork for new forms of communities or politics? Is there an ethical grounding or ideology within which to frame resistant practices? In short, we should be asking the same sorts of questions about the politics of everyday resistance that we would ask about any political tactics. The pages that follow discuss the idea of everyday resistance and then move toward an analysis of the efficacy of the practices seen in this research, their seemingly individualistic and opportunistic nature, and the extent to which they either lack or advance an ethical or moral framework for political critique.

ASSESSING EVERYDAY RESISTANCE

What is, in the end, achieved through everyday resistance? What we see among the Appalachian welfare poor is a pattern of widespread behavior that produces or supports an array of important material and symbolic results including cash and other necessities of survival, a status of autonomy, a potentially powerful collective consciousness of the struggle of welfare mothering, and a strategic opposition to and undermining of surveillance mechanisms.

The first payoff is the most straightforward; the women studied here get immediate and crucial cash or material relief through their efforts. While we have no specific findings on exactly how much that is, it is, for many of these families, what makes it possible to get by. As noted earlier, Edin's study (1993) of welfare family budgets in Chicago finds that women roughly *doubled* their resources in these ways. Obviously this is a massive and critical source of material improvement for the poor. While these women are powerless to change formal government policy regarding levels of income maintenance on welfare programs, they have effected a local and personalized change in the policy by taking charge of their own conditions. For them, their subterfuge means that allowable levels of income have been effectively raised. Through their necessarily quiet actions, they have achieved what would be one of the central goals of a more organized social movement for welfare justice: more income. This may call into question some of our fixation on the questions of whether everyday resistance can lead to more formal collective action which could then lead to "real" change. Real change is taking place in the lives of these individuals; it is not "permanent"; it is not, at least in the traditional sense, "collective"; it is not centralized reform of the state apparatus; but out at the margins, in the lives of these people, it is a change that makes a crucial difference.

The struggle for material subsistence also produces less tangible but nonetheless important results. For one, the resistant struggle works to mark and maintain a zone of autonomy and self-determination that denies the clients' status as dependent.[5] The poor are neither "wards" of the state, nor the "welfare dependent" when they are out hustling to pull together enough money to get through the month. They are partially freed from the oversight of CRIS-E and their caseworker as they enact a strategy that, whatever else may be said about it, makes them the initiators of an array of entrepreneurial pursuits. As Sarat has argued, this is a critical aspect of resistance by the welfare poor; those moments "in which welfare recipients . . . demand recognition of their personal identities and their human needs" or "establish unreachable spaces of personal identity and integrity" (Sarat 1990, 344, 347). Here, I think it is particularly important that the women are able to belie their widespread depiction as "bad mothers."

Being on welfare in the United States is to undergo an ongoing shaming and scolding: challenging the terms of that shaming by working,
by meeting needs, and by expressing their care is an important and
empowering redefinition of their public status.

There is another important sense in which the ongoing pattern of
income enhancement works as an important front and form of political resistance—this has to do with the relationship of the surveilled
subject to the surveillance state. In that the welfare administration
demands that a client open her life to them in the form of income
verification, computer matches, home visits, and other tactics in what
can only be called a full-scale surveillance assault, her secret actions
are an act of resistance to the very structure of the surveillance society. The welfare system works as hard as it can to force that secret out
of her. They will solicit "rat calls" in an attempt to get neighbors and
relatives to expose the situation. They will use computer matching
searches to check bank accounts, motor vehicle ownership, social security payments, and other searchable databases disclosing records.
*This is, in short, a power struggle over the compulsory visibility of the wel-
fare poor.* The surveillance mechanisms of the state are mechanisms of
domination which seek to force the poor into the open, prevent them
from augmenting their meager allowance with entrepreneurial pursuits, and, as a result, disempower them by closing off more and more
of the secret places in which the power of the state can be, at least
temporarily, hidden from. To the extent that the poor can maintain
those spaces, augment their income, and assert the needs and values
of their own identities, they have won a temporary but not so small
victory in the broader struggle.

These are all important political effects. Taking stock of the promising dimensions of a politics of everyday resistance does not imply
that more formal and public politics would not be a more preferen-
tial and heartening course (and one which might even be more effective at achieving some of these ends). It is also not meant to imply that
there are no costs. There are, of course, the potential for costs, risks,
and drawbacks in all political choices. Many of the actions taken by
these women are crimes and they may, after all, be caught and pun-
ished. More broadly, politicians may use evidence of "welfare fraud"
to reduce support and advance even more draconian measures of sur-

veillance. All of this may happen. But the tactical comparisons of such cost-benefit analyses overstate the extent to which relatively power-less people can pick and choose from a menu of political options. For these poor women, the pressure is on and the resources are slim. Most of their choices are shaped by social, legal, economic, and political contexts over which they have little control—these contexts, after all, are far more affected by the interests and desires of the powerful than they are by those of the sorts of people who turn to the "weapons of the weak."

THE LONELY STRUGGLE?

The traditional picture of political struggle on the part of oppressed peoples would have large groups drawing together in an expression of collective action. The idea of everyday resistance centers on what is apparently the opposite—an isolated, often secret act in pursuit of personal, even selfish, goals. But the contrasts may not be so clear. The practices of everyday resistance may not amount to a classic social movement, but what we have seen here is a form of politics that, while fragmented and dispersed, is by no means individualistic or selfish.

First, I want to suggest three ways in which the resistance seen here is not "individualistic." To be sure, these women have not locked arms in a collective march to the state capital, but there are alternatives to traditional collective action other than a full retreat into the self. Because structural and institutional arrays of power help to shape the opportunities for resistance, the resistance of those who, like the women studied here, face a largely uniform pattern of law, surveillance, domination, and need, is if not *collective*, widely shared. They may, in other words, seem to be "individualistic," but they are not *alone*, as there are legions of others experiencing the same pressures and engaging in the same actions.[6]

Second, although public cooperation is limited due to the need for secrecy regarding these often illegal activities, we found clear evidence of mutual support and cooperation among the mothers (see also Stack 1974). Most apparent is the amount of conversation and advising that goes on among clients regarding how to "work the system" or "play the game." Of the thirty-one interviews that had discussions of this issue, twenty-six women reported that they talked with other welfare clients about such things as how the system works, who the good caseworkers were, and what programs were available. Eleven of those reported getting or giving advice on how to generate extra income or get away with it without getting caught.[7] One woman even spoke of a group of neighbors who would use each other as references in required verification forms. In the face of conditions which seem to compel distrust and secrecy, we still see important signs of solidarity.

Finally, but perhaps most important, these women—like most of us—are far from alone in that their actions are designed to meet the needs and interests of their families. Like the caseworkers who use small resistant practices to help meet the needs of their clients, the mothers seen here explain their actions in terms of meeting the needs of their families. Collective action? Not in the traditional sense. But as they struggle to care for their families, they are surrounded by millions of other low-income mothers, by the occasional helping hand from a sympathetic caseworker, neighbor, or family member, and by the very needy hands of their children.

It may well be the case that the grand old strategies of social change no longer match the contexts and experiences of the welfare poor. Ewick and Silbey (1998), make the important point that new means of power and administration produce or call forth new means of resistance and opposition. Working off Foucault's arguments in *Discipline and Punish*, they suggest that more public and organized forms of opposition fit older public displays of the state's power. "By contrast, the technical, faceless, and individuated forms of contemporary power defy the possibilities of revolt or collective resistance. The spatial and temporal restructuring of the world in a disciplinary regime disables the very communities that were once the site of social disturbance" (188). The women studied here experience the welfare bureaucracy on their own—it either comes in their mailbox or they are called into an office or cubicle. They are concentrated in neither the poorhouse of old nor the modern urban housing project but spread out along the countryside, connected only by their invisible status and the equally invisible powers of the state's administrative machinery. There are few, if any, home visits, no badges, and no midnight raids. With none of these grand and visible displays of power over groups of people, it should hardly surprise us that forms of opposition and resistance are equally discreet and discrete. But it is clear that they are not *alone*. They may be isolated by the barriers and distances of modern bureaucracy and rural life, but they are not alone in experiencing the sorts of indignities, demands, and challenges that face thousands upon thousands of similarly situated women. We have much to learn about the new politics of such fragmented collectivities.

THE PRINCIPLES OF RESISTANCE

Skeptical readers of recent works on everyday resistance have noted the frequent absence of something that we might normally expect or hope to see in political struggles—principles. That is, some form of broader argument or ethic that positions and explains both the actions of the oppressed and the wrongs of the oppressors (McCann and March 1995, 218–219; Handler 1992). Isolated acts of opportunistic self-expression, it has been rightly noted, may be interesting phenomena, but they should not get more attention or significance than they deserve. In the study at hand, however, it seems clear that the patterns of everyday resistance are neither unprincipled nor unrelated to broader political critiques. While the mothers studied here don't regularly quote the Bill of Rights, many of them do—as discussed further below—make consistently principled arguments about need, duty, and obligation and explain their actions *and* their critique of the state in terms of those principles. Readily available and widely used arguments against surveillance—rights to privacy—are, in these interviews, more often than not displaced by other less abstract and decidedly less legalistic forms of complaint.

Just as practices of everyday resistance are forms of politics that eschew formal, organized, and public action and hew closely to the tangible needs, the opportunities, the experiences, and the limited resources of the rural poor, there are what might be called "everyday principles" that these women draw upon to explain their actions. These principles, like the associated practices, also hew closely to the needs, opportunities, experiences, and resources of the rural poor. As seen in the beginning of this chapter, a similar explanation for resistance marks many of these interviews. Delilah cuts hair and says that her friends sell food stamps, firewood, and scrap metal. She explains: "I think *as long as someone is using what they are doing for their home or they are buying something that their kids need, I don't see anything wrong with it*. If they are going out and they are doing it and they are boozing it up and they are using drugs, I think that's a shame."

As the epigraph to this chapter so well exemplifies—*If you have kids, you will do anything for your kids. I mean, I do. So it's not really illegal*—these stories are replete with references to mothering, child care, the need to provide for children, and the widely shared conviction that any measures taken in the interest of children are legitimate—including, for many, patently illegal actions.[8] This finding shows a shared frame of reference—an ideology of caring or parenting within a context of need—behind the seemingly discrete and apolitical actions of women in the welfare system. Although they are not united spatially, politically, or socially, the women interviewed here do share economic, institutional, and familial identities, and we can now see they also share a unified framework of language and values with which to mobilize their critiques and actions.

Many authors have now advanced the idea that an ethic or discourse of "care," emphasizing needs and interdependency, stands as an alternative to the traditional discourse of "rights" or "justice," which emphasizes individual rights and autonomy (White 2000; Tronto 1993; Gilligan 1982; Kittay and Meyers 1987; Kiss 1997). Where the latter posits an individualistic realm of legalist and rationalist calculations based on universal principles, the ethic of care emphasizes responsibilities, particular needs and differences, and compassion. From the discourse of justice, we would expect a critique of surveillance that turns on the individual's "famous formal right" to privacy (Foucault 1980, 108). From a discourse of care, however, we would expect to hear, as we do here, an emphasis on responsibility, on particular needs, on care for dependents, and on practical action to meet these concerns. As Julie White summarizes, "Care is about responsibilities rather than rights, engagement rather than abstraction, connection rather than separation; it presumes the centrality of relationship rather than individualism" (2000, 77; see also Tronto 1993, 102–104).[9]

In the history of American welfare politics, such conflicts over ways of shaping and advancing claims and issues have been recurrent and controversial. Elizabeth Bussiere writes about the impact of "maternalism" in shaping early American welfare programs (see also Ladd-Taylor 1994; Gordon 1994). Often using idealized imagery of American motherhood, maternalist politics were an important factor in the rapid spread of the mother's pension movement in the early twentieth century (Bussiere 1997, 51; Gordon 1994). "Maternalists," like contemporary advocates of "care," would typically be skeptical of arguments about universal rights that ignore the special status and specific needs related to mothering.[10] While it easy to overplay both the insularity of the competing frames and the extent of the rift between them (Kiss 1997), there has been a history of manifest conflict as a number of advocates saw grave risks in eschewing the bid for political equality and universal citizenship while advancing claims founded on women's unique and often second-class status as mother and caregiver.

In the final days of the National Welfare Rights Organization, as Elizabeth Bussiere's *(Dis)Entitling the Poor* has shown,

> the disagreements between the male strategists and the AFDC mothers went beyond tactical questions to disputes over the very language in which subsistence needs ought to be couched and legitimated. Although AFDC mothers and their children received tangible benefits from court victories, the language of welfare rights that the NWRO male leaders and LSP [Legal Services Program] lawyers had used aroused ambivalence among some members of the NWRO, the nerve center of the welfare rights movement. . . . Although finding inspiration in a natural-law understanding of human rights, the NWRO women groped for a way to think about motherhood and subsistence needs that resonated more directly with their particular experiences raising children single-handedly under daunting circumstances. The disagreements between the men and the women produced so much friction that the NWRO members ousted the male leaders in the early 1970s. (Bussiere 1997, 100–101).[11]

Thus, the language of needs, of mothering, and the demands of caring for children have been a long-standing part of American welfare politics, and tensions between these claims and a politics of rights have been apparent. As is obvious in the many examples of other women—poor, working, and middle-class—who deploy rights claims and legal action (McCann 1994; Schneider 1986; Piven and Cloward 1979), there is no fixed structural, psychological, social, or biological gendering of political discourse. There is also no impermeable wall between claims that make use of rights talk and those that make use of care talk or need talk—they emphasize different arguments and values, but there is no intrinsic or permanent separation or opposition (see also Waldron 1996). Activist attorneys have worked, for example, to construct legal rights around the needs for a healthy diet and a livable income, or children's need for a stable home (Harris 1999; Bussiere 1997; Davis 1993). Indeed, language itself is so malleable, transitory, and open-ended that we should view these women not as being driven by some structure of language or perception but, rather, as choosing from among the many terms and references that we can use to make sense of our lives and our conditions. In the conditions and contexts in which they live—united by the abusive practices in welfare administration, rural isolation, and low education discussed in the preceding chapter—it is not hard to understand how an individualistic privacy claim based in the nobility of a law would fail to make sense. In lives that are surrounded by the obligations of meeting both the needs of their dependents and the commands of those upon whom they depend, the ideal of the autonomous and rights-bearing individual must be rather far from the tip of the tongue. In many critical dimensions, then, their lives, roles, experiences, and values appear to gravitate away from the assertion of individualistic rights and toward the focus on responsibility and care. The sense of disempowerment tied to their fear, distrust, and alienation from "the law" struggles with the reality of their situations in which *something* is wrong and *something* must be done about it. Rather than publicly objecting to the infringement of their rights as citizens, they quietly meet the needs of their dependents through daily actions that defy the commands of the state.

In this setting, the discourse of need, maternalism, or care works as a critical alternative to the primary legal terms of the state, but it is important to stress that an ethic of care or maternalism is hardly a new ideological ground that frees these women from the politics of oppression. In basing claims upon the demands of mothering below the poverty line, the arguments they make here express and perhaps strengthen central elements of women's oppression. Because the sexual division of family labor on issues of care and children has been a central player in women's continuing subjugation, claims which draw upon those concerns may be an odd and troublesome part of an oppositional consciousness. But the recognition that the very terms of opposition are drawn from within the ideological frameworks of domination, underscores important characteristics of everyday politics and consciousness. Like African American slaves who drew strength from the Christian theology that was at first a doctrine of their oppressors, or like many struggling groups who have successfully drawn on legal rights that were originally the doctrines of power, privilege, and patriarchy, the women here make claims that are drawn from the terms and conditions of a world shaped by those who are more powerful. These are claims which necessarily reflect dimensions of their own oppression but which, in the endless possibilities of language and politics, also suggest new potentials for assertion and empowerment.

CONCLUSION

If you ever come down to Appalachian Ohio—or any other pocket of endemic poverty—you are not likely to find a storefront office with a sign in the window reading "Welfare Mothers Against Big Brother." But what you will find is a widespread pattern of complaint, evasion, and resistance, as welfare mothers struggle with the system that defines their condition and enforces the law through ongoing surveillance. It is a pattern of resistance that has clear results: desperately needed material benefits; the maintenance of a zone of autonomy in the face of the dependency of life on welfare; the sustenance of a shared identity of mothering; and the undermining of the surveillance mission itself.

In these ways, though they mount no grand social movement, these women engage in a realistic and necessary struggle to feed, clothe, and house themselves and their children. As Frances Fox Piven and Richard Cloward have noted,

Whatever the intellectual sources of error, the effect of equating movements with movement organizations—and thus requiring that protests have a leader, a constitution, a legislative program, or at least a banner before they are recognized as such—is to divert attention from many forms of political unrest and to consign them by definition to the more shadowy realms of social problems and deviant behavior. As a result such events as massive school truancy or rising worker absenteeism or mounting applications for public welfare or spreading rent defaults rarely attract the attention of political analysts. Having decided by definitional fiat that nothing political has occurred, nothing has to be explained, at least not in terms of political protest. (1979, 5)

This accounting of the senses in which everyday resistance advances the interests of these women is not meant to gainsay the power and importance of the surveillance program with which the poor must live. The interviews make it clear that ongoing record keeping, observation, and verification manifest a considerable and fearsome presence in their lives. Indeed, it is the very power of the surveillance mechanisms that effects the downside or costs of these forms of resistance. Several women spoke of the horrible stress of keeping their secrets and fearing apprehension; beyond the stress lies the real possibility of apprehension and sanction. Further, the subterfuge and deception necessitated by the comprehensive enforcement system means that many of the subjects here must "live a lie" and deny real aspects of their lives that are of great importance to personal dignity. The truth may be that they are not lazy, not helpless, and not involved in a pattern of broken relationships, but they must hide that truth as part of the struggle.[12] One woman, Marie, seems to have a close and loving relationship with Bill, her live-in spouse and the father of her child. But to maintain and maximize cash, food stamp, and medical benefits for herself and her young child, she spent years lying to her caseworker. She not only denied the presence of the father in her household, but said he was unknown, and described her son as the result of "a drunken one-night stand."

In resisting the truth-making of the welfare bureaucracy, Marie may have avoided direct entrapment by the system, and she certainly received a higher benefit and essential medical services for her child.

But to do so, she was forced to hide her successful relationship and the true strength and stability of her family. Therefore, this particular act of resistance inverts some of the expectations noted earlier about resistance as a moment "in which welfare recipients . . . demand recognition of their personal identities and their human needs" or "establish unreachable spaces of personal identity and integrity" (Sarat 1990, 344, 347). Marie had to deny her lover, her family, and her long-standing relationship—in some ways, she had to deny (at least to her caseworker) the very personal identity that resistance is supposed to assert. Perhaps the real tragedy of the truth-demands of the surveillance matrix is that even these moments of resistance are seized—to beat the truth, they must lie.

CHAPTER FIVE

Privacy and the Powers
of Surveillance

SOCIAL SECURITY NUMBERS threaten to rob us of our true spirit. Government computers are fundamentally evil and pose one of the primary threats to modern humanity. When welfare agencies require citizens to provide Social Security numbers for their computer matrix, they not only compel our acquiescence to evil but may well violate long-standing religious traditions.

This was the central argument against welfare surveillance that the United States Supreme Court heard in the 1986 case of Little Bird of the Snow, a member of the Abenaki Indian Tribe. When Little Bird was two years old, her parents, Stephen J. Roy and Karen Miller, applied for AFDC and food stamps in Pennsylvania. Because of new congressional mandates meant to facilitate computer matching and other forms of fraud control, the Millers were required to obtain and provide a Social Security number for all members of the family. Little Bird's parents refused, arguing that the beliefs of their tribal religion prohibited them from assigning the child a name or identity which would conflict with her tribal name. Believing that "control over one's life is essential to spiritual purity, and indispensable to 'becoming a holy person,'" they feared that "the uniqueness of the Social Security number as an identifier, coupled with the other uses of the number over which she has no control, will serve to 'rob the spirit' of [Little Bird] and prevent her from attaining greater spiritual power" (*Bowen v. Roy*, 476 U.S. 693 [1986] at 696). Further, Little Bird's father had studied the legend of Katahdin and concluded that computer technology must be resisted as one of the central evils that challenged the world.

For these reasons, Little Bird's parents refused to supply a Social Security number for their child. In response, the state terminated Little Bird's cash income under AFDC, her access to Medicaid benefits, and began proceedings to terminate her food stamps. In a 1984 bench trial before Judge Muir of the District Court for the Middle District of Pennsylvania, Little Bird's parents prevailed, but later, in a 1986 ruling, the Supreme Court reversed. Chief Justice Warren Burger argued that the needs of the state far outweighed any claims of religious freedom that the Roys had put forth. In large part, he argued, this was because of the need to meet Congress's overriding concern that fraud and error be eliminated from welfare administration. "Social Security numbers are unique numerical identifiers, and are used pervasively in these programs. The numbers are used, for example, to keep track of persons no longer entitled to receive food stamps because of past fraud or abuses of the program. Moreover, the existence of this unique numerical identifier creates opportunities for ferreting out fraudulent applications through computer 'matching' techniques" (at 710–711).

The case of Little Bird of the Snow was argued and decided within the legal framework of the First Amendment guarantees of religious freedom. The language of religious freedom was, in this setting, one way to give voice and meaning to a family's opposition to the numbering of their child, to the incumbent loss of control over her identity, and to the further capitulation to the ever-increasing power of computerized information management and control (see District Court Record). In the context of this book, the story of Little Bird stands out less as a case about religion than as a story about how we explain and confront numbering, naming, and identity within the public welfare bureaucracy and its computerized surveillance and tracking systems. Like the women studied here, Little Bird and her family found themselves in a situation of financial need and turned to the long-standing programs of the welfare state for assistance. And, like the women studied here, as they entered the computerized information bureaucracy of that system they faced immediate struggles over how the state would "see" them. Their families are renamed as "cases." Their names are replaced with Social Security numbers. Their understandings of their need and circumstances are replaced

by the state's assessment of need and eligibility. Desires, understandings, tactics, and stories that do not fit the knowledge matrix of the
state program must be pushed aside or hidden. Indeed, when Little
Bird's parents tried to refuse the renaming of their child, the government actually moved to cut off the toddler's food and medicine.

In short, for these subjects of surveillance, many of the local facets
and depictions of their lives are displaced and overrun by a unified
system of knowledge which can have little room for personal stories,
self-understandings, or tribal names. Conflict over these processes
can take many forms. Most lump it: desperate for assistance and so
overwhelmed by other concerns, the niceties of naming, identity, and
privacy seem petty and probably don't even take the shape of political problems. The parents of Little Bird in the Snow, however, took
their case to federal court and won. But when the case was appealed
and argued before the United States Supreme Court they not only
lost, they saw the Chief Justice of the United States Supreme Court
degrade their beliefs about their child's identity by comparing them
to a preference for "the size or color of the Government's filing cabinets" (*Bowen v. Roy*, 476 U.S. 693 [1986] at 700). The women studied
here forgo the trip to the Supreme Court Building and attempt to
meet the law, the bureaucracy, and the surveillance system on their
own terms and on their own turf.

Like many of the women here, the parents of Little Bird resented
their inclusion in the surveillance framework because among other
things, they saw it as a loss of control, a violation of their values, a
personal offense, and as part of a broader problem of increasing surveillance and control. The language in which Little Bird's parents
expressed these concerns—through the legend of Katahdin and their
tribal beliefs—was certainly not part of the mainstream discourse of
societal debate over surveillance, but when "translated" into the language of First Amendment law regarding freedom of religion, they
were able to mobilize their claims, albeit unsuccessfully, through the
courts. As we have seen, the women studied here also tend to speak
in a language that is foreign to the official debates—the legend of
Katahdin is replaced with stories of need, of caring, and of personal
offense.

The questions that we turn to now all center on the matter of what these women, their words, and this exploration of their experiences can bring to our efforts to understand the nature and effects of surveillance programs and the struggles which may emerge over their implementation. In the introduction, I argued that our cultural discussion of surveillance was in need of new perspectives and voices—that a droning and limiting debate over how various new policies may affect privacy rights had cabined our thinking, excluded important concerns, and truncated the possibilities of recognizing both excluded participants and new types of critiques and politics. The mission set forth, then, was to break away from the traditional venues of courts, legislatures, and policymaking and go to the "other end" of the surveillance system to talk with some of the least powerful, most heavily watched, and most rarely consulted participants in surveillance programs—the targets. We also felt it necessary to commit a different type of methodology; no survey forms, no professorial interviewers, no use of agency lists or facilities for contacts. Wanting to depart as much as possible from both the mainstream terms of the surveillance-privacy debate *and* the trappings which might tend to create an echoing of that debate or a stifling of emergent vernaculars, we sought —by having local welfare mothers undertake the loosely structured discussions—to make the interviews as much like a local conversation as possible. Such a bid can never be completely fulfilled. After all, how often would a neighbor walk through your door on a mission to talk about your experiences with welfare administration and computerization? But if we have not made it all the way to where we wanted to be, I think we have at least gotten a long way from where we were, and can now try to draw out some of the lessons of the journey.

A book such as this can be a difficult one to conclude because of the ongoing tensions between its general and far-reaching interest in things like surveillance, power, law, and resistance and the specific focus on a particular and fairly small group of welfare mothers in a largely rural region of Appalachian Ohio. Obviously, many of the experiences, claims, and concerns of this group are uncommon enough that they can not be used as exemplary cases from which to make sweeping generalizations about the overall nature of human civilization. Indeed, the recognition of the uniqueness of the settings and subjects of surveillance programs, and how this uniqueness belies and resists the totalizing tendencies of both modern surveillance programs and official discussions of them, is an important message of this work. In the pursuit of order, efficiency, and fairness, bureaucratic surveillance, welfare administration, and, in many ways, systems of law, push toward uniformity, generalization, and sameness. In the face of this, the recognition of diversity, particularity, and context are important. Having made this critique of the forms of knowledge created by contemporary systems of mass surveillance, it would hardly be appropriate to turn to such totalizing claims in these last pages.

Thus, while findings based on this group of women cannot and should not be quickly generalized to other populations in other settings of surveillance, *questions* that we can learn to ask on the basis of this study can and should be extended to other settings. In this particular setting we have seen complaints about surveillance advanced in terms of need, the obligations of mothering, and personal frustration—but it could well be other claims in other settings. As we leave this particular study behind, we want to turn and look at the broader implications. In this sense, I will argue that the specifics of the anti-surveillance complaints that we have seen here point toward a more general need to focus on context, power, and conflict—*to study the powers of surveillance as particular episodes of political domination and struggle and not as successive chapters in the legal history of the right to privacy.* The pages that follow begin with a review of the role and impact of the "right to privacy" framework, then move toward a reassessment of surveillance, its power, and the forms of scholarship and politics that best fit this reassessment.

THE RIGHT TO PRIVACY

The makers of our Constitution. . . . conferred, as against the
Government, the right to be let alone—the most comprehensive
of rights and the right most valued by civilized men.
    Olmstead v. U.S. 277 U.S. 438 [1928], Brandeis dissenting

Heeding these alternative ways of thinking and speaking about surveillance policy can both add to our understanding of the variety of local languages within our political culture and make a contribution to mainstream policy debate by bringing in new voices, insights, and critiques. The prevailing language of the right to privacy provides a powerful and often respected set of claims through which to express opposition to surveillance policy. Through its assertion of a protected, nonpublic zone around the individual, and its valuing of the ideas of autonomy and repose, the privacy paradigm has much apparent potential as a language with which to frame our critiques of surveillance policy.

We certainly hear a lot about it. Again and again, newspapers, television news shows, and foundation-backed special reports issue clarion calls that the right of privacy is threatened by new surveillance technology. Again and again, public opinion polls show widespread support for an abstract right to privacy. Again and again, the courts confront the privacy issues, whether through a Fourth Amendment framework, a claim under one of the legislative privacy or information acts, or some other element of the law. In short, the language of privacy rights is the only show in town when it comes time to talk about surveillance policy. And (also in short), there are a number of good reasons to suggest that it may be time to broaden and deepen the terms upon which we discuss surveillance policy. The discussion which follows addresses a few critiques that have been raised about problems that seem to be intrinsic to the idea of the right to privacy, that is, they are concerns about the idea and implications of privacy itself—its individualistic premises, its isolationist ethic, and the odd and problematic vision of both our social life and the nature of surveillance that it often implicitly asserts.

But I forward these critiques somewhat tentatively, because of my feeling that, for one, privacy is an important, widely shared, and needed value in our times. Despite its crimes of omission and commission, the idea of a right to privacy raises important questions about the surveillance state and should, therefore, not be lightly gainsaid. But, these critiques about the intrinsic problems about the language of privacy rights are also tentative because, simply put, *all* such critiques of language should be tentative—none of the "meaning" in the worlds of language and politics is truly intrinsic. Words, laws, ideas are important parts of cultural history and are thus not entirely open-ended, but they are, to a continually surprising degree, both malleable and filled with potential for new applications. Anyone who has followed, for example, the twisting history of the idea of due process in American law knows that other symbolic constructions like "rights," or the idea of "privacy," can be extended and transformed to take on different meanings and implications in different times and places.

For these reasons, I think it is important to use the results of this study to speak to not just what some of the problems with privacy are, but, more importantly, what some of the silences of the current debate are. What and who is missing? How can we expand both our conversations and the participation in our conversations about surveillance policy? Thus, the goal here is not to replace or discard the important ideas implied by the idea of privacy, but to broaden our discussion with terms and concerns that are often muted in the current debates.

THE PROBLEMS OF PRIVACY

The limits to the privacy rights paradigm are well-recognized in the academic literature, particularly in the critical writings of authors from feminist, communitarian, and critical legal studies perspectives. Much of this work centers on the fact that the privacy concept is historically and theoretically wed to a hyper-individualist understanding of life and society; a framework which has been called to task for both its historical inaccuracies and its contemporary political implications (see Regan 1995; Glendon 1991; Copelon 1989; Allen 1988). Like classic theorists who begin their social visions with unfettered individuals strolling out of the wilderness, bearing their natural rights, and applying their previously autonomous selves to a new community, many privacy writers posit a society of lonesome individuals who have, apparently, developed self and outlook in a wilderness free from others. Definitions of privacy echo this hyper-individualism—as one prominent essay put it: "an individual enjoys *perfect* privacy when he is completely inaccessible to others" (Gavison 1980, 428).[1] Or, as it went in the famous Brandeis dissent, privacy is "the right to be let alone." From this starting point, an analysis can proceed to say that a violation of privacy has occurred when the individual's solitude, anonymity, or secrecy is violated (Gavison, 1980; Nock 1993). We are presented with an individual seeking protection from a surveillance program that would violate the "natural" state of solitude by taking a snaphot of an item or behavior that the individual would prefer to hide.

The prevailing understandings, then, would tend to frame the individual as existing in a free and natural state prior to the "visitation" by a surveillance program and as returning to that state of privacy and solitude once the observation is completed. From this perspective, "privacy" is something that can be "restored" once the cameras or computers are turned off. But what seems clear, from both this study and other efforts to assess the ongoing impact of surveillance programs, is that the impact of surveillance is perhaps even more insidious than a disruption of natural solitude—as permanent frames of reference, assessment, and decision, surveillance programs shape our lives and understandings in ways that we may not even fully recognize. To what extent are the worried sleepless nights, the senses of guilt and fear, the desperate rationalizations of necessary rule-breaking, the near-paranoid concern for what others see, merely passing conditions for the women studied here? The sometimes numbed awareness of ongoing assessment, calculation, and measurement which besets not just these women, but most participants in advanced industrial cultures, works as a form of power which shapes our behavior and consciousness, and, therefore, what could only be called "the self." To the extent, then, that the privacy paradigm relies on and maintains the idea of the autonomous individual and the idea of surveillance as mere visitation, it risks a massive misrepresentation of the full impact of surveillance in our lives. The positioning of extensive and ongoing surveillance in the modern state promises to recast the citizen into the frames and terms of bureaucratic analysis and translate our ongoing actions into tactics of compliance, evasion, and above all, calculation.

Other significant critiques have been made as well. Communitarian Mary Ann Glendon (1991) argues that the discourse of privacy is also a discourse of abandonment and irresponsibility. Referring to the court's practice of protecting maternal autonomy in reproductive decision-making (most notably regarding the right to choose an abortion), Glendon argues that the idea of individual autonomy continues past birth and includes the right of the mother to be stuck with inadequate housing, inadequate social support, and inadequate enforcement of paternal responsibilities. In her view, the social world defined by the individualistic value of privacy is an uncaring world of neglect in which the most needy and dependent are cut off from the support and potential of a broader community. This critique of privacy resonates with a broader critique of the ethic of rights itself, the legalistic vocabulary within which the idea of a privacy right is understood. Selma Sevenhuijsen succinctly describes a key element in the critique of rights: "arguments made on the basis of this ethic, certainly if they arise from the liberal tradition of the social contract, generally suppose a detached, self-sufficient, independent or atomistic individual, primarily engaged in pursuing his self interest; a being who is fundamentally egocentric, living in competition with and in fear of other individuals" (Sevenhuijsen, 1998, 11–12). In important ways, Sevenhuijsen, like Mary Ann Glendon, exaggerates the individualistic nature of rights claims as a general category—although there are certainly strong individualistic tendencies in liberal legal systems, there are also numerous instances in which rights mobilization has served solidaristic and community oriented ends. But when it comes to the *right of privacy*—the right to be let alone—Sevenhuijsen's comments ring true.

The potential importance of these points takes more than a single form. Priscilla Regan's *Legislating Privacy* (1995) argues that the individualistic nature of the privacy claim makes it a weak antisurveillance force in legislative battles; since new surveillance initiatives are almost always in pursuit of broad social goods like reducing crime, drug use, or welfare fraud, the lonely and selfish claim to privacy just can't stand up. For the study at hand, which centers on women who are embedded in the care and nurturance of young families, it was frequently the case that this ethic of a "detached, self-sufficient, independent or atomistic individual, primarily engaged in pursuing his self-interest" is, quite simply, nonsensical. With almost no relevance or bearing for the conditions of their daily lives, such an ethic was able to do little to help them make sense of their world or take action upon it. Instead, as we have seen, they voice their response to surveillance in terms which came directly from their daily experiences—personal relations, need, and the obligation to care.

In this light, there appears to be a strong possibility that the privacy rights language may serve to exclude a significant portion of the population for whom the idea of the private individual is just silly—people, many of them women and others who are deeply involved in family life, caregiving, or other relations involving significant dependency and interdependency. To the extent that the institutionalized mainstream languages of surveillance and privacy appear nonsensical to citizens like this, or fail to recognize their concerns, the languages work as vehicles of exclusion. And to the extent that these languages discount and hamper what many of us would want to say about surveillance, their continued monopolization of the public discourse may serve to both suppress and distort public dialogue on these important issues. In a less formal version of the "English only" laws which seek to exclude many of our more recent immigrants from public life in some areas of the country, the "privacy only" approach to the problem of surveillance may serve to sideline both people and the contributions and claims that they would bring to the table.

Our nation is adopting widespread policies of surveillance and control with either a barely stifled yawn or even muted applause. Despite consistent poll results showing concern about something called "privacy," technologies which would have once looked Orwellian now mark the face of our social landscape (see also Davies 1999). In retailing and consumerism, in the workplace, in education, in finance, law enforcement, health care, and other areas, the types of information systems seen here are being rapidly embraced as the central mode of administrative management. Some of the reason for our yawns and applause is surely that many of these policies bring some benefits to us. Just as many of the women here appreciated the fact that their checks normally came more promptly with the new computer system, many of us appreciate simplifications created by more efficient systems of administration in equally important areas of our lives.

Convenience is certainly part of the answer. But it also seems clear from the conversations studied here, that when given a chance to talk about surveillance policies in everyday terms, people *are* concerned. And when we looked at types of oppositional activity which do not match the profiles for "normal" politics, we saw widespread resistance. Perhaps more Americans should be invited to engage in conversations about the multifaceted and diverse effects of surveillance that we have seen here—the degradation, the loss of control, the implied suspicion, the feelings of being just a number, the anxiety over errors or subterfuges being caught, the fear of malevolence or incompetence on the part of surveillance practitioners, the fear of breaking rules or departing from norms that are unknown, and, especially, the need or desire to break the rules. Perhaps we might engage in more substantive policy debates as an alternative to the abstractions of a privacy right. Do we not create an odd politics when conversations that are really about the complex and very tangible effects that surveillance and centralized administration have on our personal power to control our bodies, income, and behavior all get boiled down to an ongoing discussion of "the right to privacy"? [2]

The promise of witnessing the critique seen here—a critique coming out of the everyday politics of need and care—is not necessarily that the ideas of need and care seen in chapter 4 can serve as some broadly relevant way to speak about the politics of surveillance. The point is that by paying attention to what people are saying and doing about these important public policy issues, we can build better and more inclusive accounts and understandings of societal concerns. "Privacy" is a very important and meaningful thing to lots of people. This study suggests that meeting needs and taking care of others is, too. And so, it seems clear, is a sense of personal dignity. By moving away from the discursive monopoly of the privacy paradigm we might begin to hear about things like need and care, or religious objections, or fears of concentrated powers, and other unimagined claims as well. And we might, as we add these differently critical voices and ideas to the conversation, begin to learn more about the politics of surveillance.

The Powers of Surveillance

Conversations about the idea of surveillance often bear fascinating parallels to conversations about the nature of the social sciences. Both, after all, are enterprises for studying and trying to understand events and conditions in the social world. Descriptions of surveillance parallel the vision of the social sciences that is still held by some—a vision that would ordinarily fall under the tag of "naive positivism." In this view, a surveillance system or the social scientist are neutral observers who, without bias or predisposition, visit upon the natural world of social relations, take a silent snapshot of reality, and depart with nary a footprint in the sand. It is the snapshot, not the history, premises, or heart and soul of the observer, that is the definitive text and source of analysis. The observer is practically an innocent by-stander, or a messenger who delivers the news from "reality" to the audience at hand.

But, really, hardly anyone believes this. Not even the proverbial snapshots themselves get this unproblematic treatment. As John Tagg has argued in his study of the photograph: "We have to see that *every* photograph is the result of specific and, in every case, significant distortions which render its relation to any prior reality deeply problematic and raise the question of the determining level of the material apparatus and the social practices within which photography takes place" (1988, 2). Most of the social sciences, too, now recognize that their ways of knowing and seeing are always profoundly affected by the apparatus that they use and the social practices that surround them, not to mention the languages that they speak, the priorities that they hold, and the terrain from which they work. Observation, theorizing, and exploration in the social sciences are now most frequently understood to be creative projects which limit, shape, and give meaning to the worlds that they study.

But this recognition, I would argue, often fails to inform discussions of surveillance technique and policy. There persists a Cronkitian "and that's the way it is" mentality in our thinking about things like computer matching, drug testing, and video surveillance: again and again these quite partial and problematic fragments of knowledge are privileged as definitive forms of evidence in an authoritative world-view. But once we leave the naive positivist's world of facts, accuracy, and the mythical snapshot behind, surveillance programs such as these must be understood as more than mere peepholes. They are profoundly political actions which both build and advance particular ways of understanding our world and what occurs in it.

A surveillance program of the sort that we have been discussing normally includes some set of norms, rules, or regulations and some mechanism for observing and testing the extent of an individual's compliance with those guidelines. Much of the most important "politics of surveillance" takes place in the social and political processes of constructing the guidelines that shall be used. Often, as seen in the historical examples that opened the first chapter, the nature and availability of surveillance technology itself works to shape those norms. In the case of employee drug testing, as another example, company personnel policies in the 1980s had to be reworded so that it was not only a violation to use or be influenced by illegal drugs in the workplace, but to test positive for the presence of evidence of illegal drug use. This change was necessary because drug tests were unable to measure actual impairment or even recency of use; they could only show that the body had at some point been exposed to the substances. Here, the applicable laws were rewritten to accord with the nature and limits of the available technology. The norm was no longer "be straight at work," it was "do not test positive for drug use," which normally translated into "do not use illegal drugs at all."

In other cases, it may be less the available technologies that shape the norms than the political and social pressures of a given historical moment. Continuing the preceding example, in the War on Drugs hysteria of the 1980s, the much-touted push for workplace drug testing bizarrely excluded alcohol, by any measure the drug that causes the greatest amount of mayhem in the American workplace. Since the technology for alcohol testing was well-developed, affordable, and widely available, one can only turn to political and social processes to explain the odd decision. Here we might look at, among other things, decisions about who and what was really the target of surveillance programs, the existence of political pressure from the alcohol industry, social practices and acceptances distinguishing between legal and illegal drugs, and prejudices about the users of each (Gilliom 1994).

Turning back to welfare policies, scholars frequently and with good reason contrast the old age pension with Aid to Families with Dependent Children. Both are provisions of the Social Security act of 1935. Both seek to combat poverty by using government programs to redistribute money to those deemed in need—they are both, in short, "welfare." But there the similarities stop. In the Social Security old age pension, there is an assumption of eligibility and need that is determined by age and administered through a relatively simple and noninvasive program of application and distribution. With AFDC, however, regulations were written to continue the old widows-and-orphans funds that had been developed at the county and state level in the first decades of the twentieth century. Here there was a sharp emphasis on determining and verifying eligibility on the basis of demonstrable and verified need and verified moral worth. No applicant of the old age pension was ever asked about how many lovers they had taken in past years or if they were making any extra money through babysitting. Nor was the nation's banking system surveyed for evidence that an applicant might have a little money salted away. Welfare for the elderly was a privileged form of assistance which in common practice would not even be thought of as "welfare"; AFDC however, was "the dole" and the shame, stigma, and surveillance that comes with it reveals the moral ordering of the society. It is, in this light, quite telling that the government's proudest surveillance programs were aimed at ferreting out and eliminating fraud in its welfare programs rather than ferreting out and assisting any hungry children, needy families, or unmet health needs that our welfare programs had failed.

In sum, surveillance programs should not be viewed as mere techniques or tools for neutral observation. They are, rather, expressions of particular historical and cultural arrays of power—program goals, criteria, and data sources all express social, political, and technological conditions of the times. Unpacking the histories of particular surveillance programs, as chapter 1 attempted to do, can help us to see the particular structures and currents and the ways in which they form. Such an emphasis on the prejudices and injustices that exist in the political and social processes fueling the design of a surveillance system can help to pierce and challenge the neutral technocratic guise into which so many programs slip once they are in place.

One of the most surprising things about the ongoing coverage of surveillance in the popular media is that in the media's rush to quote a privacy advocate on the latest loss to privacy, we hardly ever hear about what must be one of the most important issues of all: the ongoing shifts of power and domination inherent in the tooling and retooling of surveillance programs. The rise of CRIS-E and the number matching programs, the drug-testing policies, credit reporting, health insurance and banking data swaps, and other recent innovations manifests a massive transformation in the relationship between individuals and the institutions in their lives. Although they fight back, the welfare mothers studied here lost a great deal of the autonomy and control that they could otherwise have over their personal lives—they lost options, they lost security, and many of them lost money. County officials and caseworkers also lost power and autonomy as more and more decision-making and review was pulled into the automated framework of the online Client Information System. There can be no question, then, that the turn to the computerization of surveillance and administration represents a revolutionary shift in administrative power of the state system. As similar trends occur in the workplace, the schools, the streets, and the markets for things like insurance and healthcare, it seems remarkable that the American discussion of surveillance is virtually silent on the transformations of power that are manifest in these changes.

Despite these silences on the surface, an acute awareness of the power of vision can be seen at almost every level and context of human life. From a young child's effort to hide some candy pilfered from a forbidden kitchen cabinet, to biblical awe of an all-seeing God, to the idea that even Santa Claus "knows when you've been sleeping [and] knows when you're awake," we know, confront, and are awed by, the politics of vision. Sometimes we seek attention, sometimes we avoid it, sometimes we don't care, but there is little doubting that much of our lives involves concern for and management of how others see us. But what is the power of vision?

One of the powers of surveillance that we see here is the power to forbid. It attempts to deny or forbid autonomy and security through its search for violations of the code and its fusions with the sanctioning power of either the welfare authorities or the criminal laws of the state. We see this in the stern warnings of the application forms, the posters promising jail time to the wicked, and the news stories of convicted welfare cheats being brought to trial. The women studied here, who are almost uniformly compelled to violate at least some aspects of the law, are frightened by these powers and their capacity to forbid and punish. Surveillance is, then, a part of traditional forms of control. Along with the club, the gun, and the prison, it can work as part of a system for the relatively simple production of compliance through fear.

Traditional ideas about power tended to stop here—to see power as a tool with which those who possess it can control those who do not. But other powers of surveillance center on its capacity as a creative force—communicating norms, channeling behavior, and shaping people. Michel Foucault's visionary coupling of his ideas about the nature of power, knowledge, and the citizen-subject charted a new course for much of the work being done on surveillance policy. Foucault argues that power is far more diffuse, circulating, and creative than what is suggested by the older images of the violent state. His different works on sexuality, madness, and penology attempt to explore how cultural and institutional dynamics in these areas work to create new understandings of humanity and identity.

For the study of surveillance, the most tangible and frequently discussed aspect of Foucault's work was the book *Discipline and Punish* (1979), and more particularly, his chapter on the panopticon, the innovative prison designed by Jeremy Bentham in 1791. The breakthrough manifest in the panopticon was its capacity to use vision and spatial relations as the primary means of control. The panopticon was designed as a cylindrical building with the individual prison cells built into the outer wall of the cylinder. At the center, or hub, of the cylinder was a guard tower. All parts of all cells were open to the view of the guards at all times, making any abnormal behaviors subject to immediate detection. At the core of the theory of panoptic power is the idea that the prisoners, under the perpetual eye, are experiencing a normalizing process, or a disciplining, through which they lose the opportunity, capacity, and will to deviate. The hope is, as Foucault put it, that they "internalize the gaze" so that the operation of power becomes cheaper, easier, and more effective. As power grows more and more familiar to the constantly watched individuals, they are increasingly disciplined to the norm and thus, over time, lose the capacity and characteristics of autonomy.

Foucault imagines the power of surveillance as something that is crafty, circulating, smart, and overwhelming. Under its power, we will almost inevitably succumb to the normalizing process which denies us any chance for truly autonomous existence. But another important work, *Seeing like a State* (1998) by James Scott, suggests that the power of surveillance is often an almost bumbling power which miscasts the world and its inhabitants, overlooks essential points of information, and helps generate the seeds of its own resistance through its ongoing misreadings of local knowledge. Scott argues that modern states must produce knowledge and information to guide their various missions of social intervention and design. To do so, they must both simplify a complex social reality and rewrite the terms of that reality to fit the terms of the intervention: a mass of people becomes a list, and last names and even street addresses are introduced as ways of organizing and knowing the population. A wilderness becomes a forest with full analysis of species and harvesting schedules. Scott argues that modern statecraft requires these systems of knowledge and that, further, it is these very systems of knowledge which doom statecraft to failure. The failure of statecraft is virtually guaranteed, he argues, because the systematic state knowledge necessarily omits or overruns the sorts of local and varied knowledge and practices that are inherent to any setting. Since these local forms of knowledge would be essential to the success of state planning, their omission essentially guarantees failure, as well as conflict and resistance from subjected peoples.

Scott's comprehensive study of case after case of states taking control of and overrunning local forms of knowledge and practice with rationalized frameworks of knowledge makes a crucial contribution to the way we think about the sorts of bureaucratic surveillance studied here. Scott, like Foucault, wants to think of the state not just as passively watching, but as actively depicting and creating (Scott also pays much more attention to the formally understood "state" than Foucault). Scott's state, just like Foucault's panopticon, is not just observing the subjects, it is attempting to make them over in its vision and it does this through its actions of observation, depiction, and intervention. And while Foucault is at best suggestive of the possibility and capacity of resistance, the local populace in Scott's work resists—relying on their more meaningful and tried local practices and knowledges in the face of the state interventions.

In the case at hand, this attempt to learn something about the role of surveillance as a form of power in the lives of welfare mothers in rural Appalachian Ohio, it seems that both understandings are true. The state's efforts to "see" the poor through the starkly bureaucratic and rationalist lens of its surveillance programs produces, as we discussed in chapter 1, a weird and partial picture of the poor. Although hundreds of questions are asked of either the poor or their data sets, the few real questions are relatively simple—are they eligible for a program, how much help can they get, and are they trying to cheat us? The surveillance system seeks to gauge truth and compliance by using officially recorded sources of income and savings in a data set which is awesome in its capacity to measure recorded events anywhere in the nation, but laughable in its blindness to unrecorded income, barter, and trade—activities which have been seen as one of the defining characteristics of Appalachian culture (Halperin 1990). While the state seeks to outlaw these practices through tax laws and welfare regulations, they persist. As Scott would expect, these vibrant local practices display and maintain the indigenous characteristics of the land and its people. Things like haircuts, child care, woodcutting, extended family support systems, and casual day labor were important parts of the Appalachian economy long before the New Deal and Great Society programs arrived, and they continue despite the state's best effort to make them succumb to it commands.

But what of Bentham's hope that under the gaze of the panopticon, the capacity and even the idea of wrongdoing would disappear? Part of the answer is that the panopticon has an exaggerated prefix— that no power will ever be able to see and know *all*—that blind spots and omissions will always exist and that local conditions and peoples will almost always assert their own terms and understandings. But the other, bleaker, part of the answer is that these are a diminished people. While many of them may complain about their caseworkers and the bureaucracy, they also fear them and bring few formal complaints— afraid to rock the boat or, in one's particularly apt phrase, "stir up shit." While most of them have a few tricks for improving their families' standard of living, they have far less then they used to: the possibility of receiving dual benefits in different counties or states; of hiding income or savings through a simple lie; of selling or trading food stamps; and other practices have all been eliminated by the increasing perfection of the state's capacity to see.

What was also striking was the frequent emergence of guilt and regret over the rule breaking and this is, perhaps, an important sign of the "internalizing of the gaze" that Foucault writes of when he discusses the long-term impact of a successful panopticon. Where many of us would see a parent skirting or overlooking petty rules for the benefit of their children as justifiable, if not a cause for pride, many of the women here seemed to have real regrets for their actions—in the words of one "I feel real bad." Another: "it makes me feel like a dog." Cultural ideals about truth and falsehood, advertising campaigns about the evils of welfare fraud, threats both implicit and explicit in the welfare department's forms, the awareness of the risk of detection and punishment, all in the long term combine to create an environment in which, perhaps, someday, people will lose the capacity to imagine wrongdoing, even when that "wrongdoing" could be seen as "rightdoing" from a slightly different perspective.

And it is this struggle between what is right and wrong that, in the end, may be one of the most important reasons that we need to confront and understand the powers of systematic surveillance. In a sloppier, fragmented, disconnected world, there are—for better and worse—infinite local possibilities for struggles and conversations over moral and political choices. But the most important requirement of centralized surveillance and administration is that norms and guidelines must be identified and enforced. Conversation and debate must stop as administration and enforcement begin. "Opposition" becomes "noncompliance" and "resistance" becomes "cheating." "Fair hearings" may be granted over procedural terms, but substantive choices over what matters and what doesn't, that which qualifies and that which disqualifies, that which is bad and that which is good, become institutionalized and widely and rigidly asserted over large populations.

We are in the midst of a technological and institutional revolution in technologies of surveillance. With the massive changes in the capacity, speed, and ubiquity of computer systems, the processing of massive amounts of information has become possible for the first time in human history. With the scientific development of ways to "read" numerous traces or markers of behavior or whereabouts—DNA tests and drug tests, for example—a lab test or computer match, rather than a human being, can bear authoritative witness to an act which, perhaps, no one ever saw. With the bureaucratic and institutional enhancements of the ability to trace people—such as the nearly universal use of the Social Security number, vehicle identification numbers, digital and DNA fingerprints—the administrative capacity for monitoring and identification has increased dramatically. And with governmental and private authorities stepping up requirements for the use of systematic markers and indices—such as the Social Security number or a credit card number—for almost any transaction, the institutional capacity for monitoring is markedly enhanced.

The technological, scientific, and administrative infrastructure for comprehensive and ongoing scrutiny of human affairs is thus well established and few of us can now go through an ordinary life without being conscious of it. Surveillance may be ongoing, like credit reporting, subject to chance encounter, like a police officer with a radar gun or detection animal, or in the form of a triggered or random investigation, like an IRS audit or a workplace drug test. But whatever the form, when the surveillance capacity of authorities in the areas of education, criminal law enforcement, insurance, health care, finance, social services, taxation, motor-vehicle use, and other realms are considered in their combined impact, there can be little doubt that the powers and politics of information have hit the big time. As large-scale data sets gather and fix more and more information about both individuals and groups, and that information is shared across institutions, the possibilities of evasion and noncompliance will be inevitably reduced. This dramatic increase and concentration in the power and capacity of centralized authorities to assert norms, monitor behavior, and enforce compliance may well mark one of the most important transformations of power as we enter the twenty-first century.

In the End . . .

This book has tried to accomplish two closely related tasks. First, it has tried to make the case for a rejuvenation and recrafting of the tools, terms, and ideas with which we both study and confront the increasingly important impact of surveillance in our lives. Second, it has tried to demonstrate with its findings and analysis some of the ways and means through which new forms for study and confrontation could occur. Each element of this book has been an important part of this dual endeavor. We began with a self-conscious effort to "escape" the prevailing frames and terms of formal law, privacy rights, and policy analysis by going to the seldom visited homes of people who are the *targets* of surveillance, not the originators, the certified critics, or the professional analysts. As we began to study these people, in chapter 1, we self-consciously sidestepped a historical analysis of privacy rights, or a policy analysis of welfare expenditure and fraud. Rather we studied the historical terms through which the surveillance of the poor has developed as part of the broader development of the welfare state and the gender and class politics that have helped define it. Through this study of the emergent structure of welfare surveillance, we set the stage for a subsequent focus on the micropolitics of daily life as a welfare mother. In chapters 2 and 3, we looked at the way that these women experience, explain, and complain about welfare bureaucracy and surveillance and, in so doing, we were able to see the relationships between their apparently individual experiences and complaints and the broader patterns seen in both the group as a whole and the historical terms and structures of welfare administration.

It is here that we began to see a story that is both tragic and heartening. The tragedy, of course, is that these women seem to be so far removed from the empowering ideas of rights, the dignified claims of citizen privacy, and the expressions of public outrage that should accompany such treatment. But we did not, of course, find complete acquiescence: in the absence of conventional ideology and politics, we found patterns of critique and action drawn from the experiences and conditions of everyday life and directed toward meeting the impact of the surveillance bureaucracy in the terms that mattered most. In chapter 4, we explored how this everyday critique and resistance was an important and productive form of politics advancing the daily needs of the poor, building and reflecting collective identity, and both working from and strengthening a principled and ethical ideology.

Overall, then, this exploration of the politics of surveillance has tried to put four key elements at the center of analysis: the historical structuring of power and domination in the institutions and practices surrounding the participants in a surveillance regime; the daily experiences and conditions of those most intensely affected by surveillance programs; the local and, perhaps, unconventional terms and practices through which these people explain and address their situation; and the ways in which these local terms and practices, in their nature, if not their specific content, can instruct our broader efforts to understand and respond to surveillance.

In the end, the bottom line has been to resist the appeal of the privacy rights paradigm, so that we could examine welfare surveillance as a particular episode in ongoing relationships of power and domination along the well-established fault lines of race, class, and gender. New forms of surveillance are, indeed, new techniques of power which bring important new features to our political and social world. But they are techniques of power that come to and from a political and social world defined by long-standing relations and patterns. We need to resist the temptations to which we so often yield, to frame "surveillance" within the transcendent abstractions of the surveillance-privacy debate, or to isolate the topic and its startling new technologies as unique and removed from the ongoing dynamics of political struggle. For the story seen here, while featuring some new techniques and some innovative coping mechanisms, is a very old story—poverty, domination, and the endless struggles of everyday people.

EPILOGUE

THIS BOOK HAS ATTEMPTED to study the politics of surveillance in ways and places that depart from the more conventional languages and settings. By avoiding the terms of the bureaucratic agencies, eschewing a "law first" focus, and undertaking in-depth field interviews administered by and with rural welfare mothers, we have hoped to get past some of the formalities, barriers, and preconceptions of language to get at the more casual, informal, and personal terms of everyday social life. No such effort can ever be completed. Understandings are always limited by the gulf of experience and context that exist between author, subjects, readers, and other participants in the exercise. No matter how many times we pore over the interview notes or listen to the tapes, the gaps created by life, experience, and subjectivity always remain.

In the summer that I struggled to finish this project, something happened which both reduced the gaps and illuminated the spaces that remained: a police surveillance program led to an armed invasion and search of my home and placed my wife and me under ongoing suspicion and investigation for the commission of federal felonies. The days, weeks, and months in which these events unfolded were not only times that tried the soul of our family, they were a rapid, intense, and visceral education into the politics of surveillance, privacy, power, and the law. For these reasons, the next several pages depart from the "regularly scheduled programming" to offer a brief firsthand account of the events in question. It is a telling which will, in the sharing, offer up a large-scale violation of my privacy, but no more so than has been done to the women whose interviews we dissected in the preceding pages. It is also a telling which will, for a few pages, be surprisingly personal for an academic work; post hoc editing and rewriting have been minimized in an effort to maintain the tone of these largely contemporaneous journal notes. Such an approach is called for. The ethnographic bent upon which this book is founded, after all, rejects the universalizing knowledge claims of the detached scholar, in order to seek forms of understanding that are embedded in the local perspectives of specific contexts and people. I just hadn't planned on things getting quite so personal.

•

My family lives in an aging farmhouse situated in a small valley of about sixty rough, hilly, and mostly wooded acres. We are about ten miles from the city of Athens, Ohio, on a poorly maintained dirt road, and are neighbored on all sides by large holdings of forested private and public land. Because of the forests, the hot summers, and the endemic poverty, our region of the state is known for its marijuana cultivation. And because of this, late each summer, those of us who live out in the rural parts of the county brace ourselves for persistent flyovers by the black helicopters of the State Bureau of Criminal Identification and Investigation. Working with ground forces provided by local sheriff's departments, the helicopters freely search yards, fields, forests, and gardens and call in truckloads of deputies to undertake the raids on any plantings they find.

In August of 1999, while we were out of town, they came to our house. For me, it started with a phone call.

"John, it's Larry. Hey look, I have some really really bad news. We've heard from Jenny and Mark [our house-sitters] that helicopters have landed at your farm, that they have found a lot of marijuana plants, and that they are getting a warrant to search your house. The 'copters circled around the back fields and hills, then landed, and then some guys showed up in trucks and four-wheelers and took off through your back yard. They wouldn't let Jenny back in the house, so she couldn't get your phone number. We finally tracked down your parents' phone number through Don. When Mark got home, he asked if they were free to leave. Eventually, the sheriff said that they were, so they left and we don't know what is going on."

I got my friend's phone number, thanked him for going through the effort to find us and hung up. I told my hosts that there seemed to be a drug bust going on at my house. I said that there should be nothing to worry about because we certainly hadn't been growing any marijuana and that there was to our knowledge nothing illegal in the house, the outbuildings, or on our land. We were innocent of wrongdoing and had no reason for concern.

I was lying. Not about growing the pot. That was the truth (and this stalwart critic of surveillance would soon consider taking a polygraph to prove it). When I lied, and I would be unable to sustain it for more than a few minutes, it was with the assertion that we had nothing to worry about. I stepped outside and told my wife, Amy. The jolt that knocked her body and the look on her face showed that she wouldn't buy any lies about having nothing to worry about. The torso full of fear and tension that would be my constant companion for the days to come moved in. The almost unbearably high-speed rush of thoughts, counter thoughts, arguments, and scenarios that would become my consciousness began.

Why the worry? We were innocent of wrongdoing. We were middle-class and could afford an attorney, at least for a while. We were white and we were well connected to the large university that dominates our county. "Our county." That was the rub. The last five years in our county had seen an almost endless string of corruptions, excesses, and embarrassments among the law enforcement agencies and the offices of the county prosecutor. For a sleepy rural university town it had also seen a startling militarization of the "War on Drugs," with no-knock midnight searches over small amounts of marijuana, aggressive property forfeiture policies, the widespread use of paid non-police informants, lockdown searches of high schools by dogs and black-hooded agents (no drugs found), and other manifestations of zero tolerance policing. In executing their war, the local police had committed strings of rights violations. They had searched whole fraternity buildings on the basis of a warrant for one room, made body-cavity searches of individuals seen smoking something that may have been a marijuana cigarette, and used blatantly pretextual traffic stops to pursue suspected vehicles. (Picture a "routine" left-of-center traffic stop in which several squad cars surround the vehicle, guns are drawn, and the driver is forced to walk backward with hands on head to be handcuffed and ticketed.) Judges had been suppressing evidence in case after case. In one search of a family home, a large sum of money disappeared and the sheriff's deputies were the key suspects. A special prosecutor had to be brought in to indict and try a deputy for theft and his supervisor for perjury. The former was acquitted, then immediately resigned; the latter took a plea bargain at the last minute, but faced no serious disciplinary action and remains on duty. (The judge seemed to give his view on the situation when fining the homeowner for illegal distribution of prescription drugs: he reduced the fine by the exact amount that had disappeared in the search.)

There were other problems too—indeed, they permeated the law enforcement system. Around the time that the county prosecutor and one of his assistant prosecutors began suing each other over a personal relationship gone wrong, a previous prosecutor was caught in an apparent effort to file false ballots in a federal election. He took a plea bargain and received a two-year license suspension from the state supreme court. More recently, the marshall of a nearby town was caught seizing evidence from citizens and selling it for his own profit, cash has turned up missing from the sheriff's evidence vault, two on-duty police officers in a neighboring town were apprehended using and selling prescription painkillers, sans prescription, and a sheriff's deputy resigned amid charges that he was sexually involved with a fourteen-year-old girl.

Angry and Disgusted

In short, for a sleepy little county in the middle of nowhere, we had a surprising number of troubles and deeply troubled people in our law enforcement system. Hadn't people noticed? They had. In the face of a long string of excesses and abuses that took place under the leadership of a particularly Rambo-esque commander of a federally funded narcotics task force, an uprising of civil libertarians, students, townspeople, and attorneys brought the issue to a head. There were news articles and letters to the editor, poster campaigns, nonviolent protests, and public debates over police tactics and citizen rights. Finally, in a major triumph for the civil libertarians (and clear indication of how bad things were), the county council actually voted to *refuse federal grant money*—I am not making this up—in order to get the narcotics task force out of the county. The county prosecutor who oversaw the task force was angry and disgusted. The county sheriff was angry and disgusted. The city police chief was angry and disgusted.

But we celebrated. One of the central activists in this struggle with law enforcement run amok was Amy King, the president of the regional chapter of the American Civil Liberties Union and my partner for life. She had been quoted on the radio and in the newspaper, she had organized the opposition, she had attended the council meetings, she had—perhaps most dangerously—assisted the special prosecutor who indicted members of the sheriff's department. For her work, the American Civil Liberties Union of Ohio had feted her as a Beacon of Liberty at the annual meeting and national ACLU president Nadine Strossen had congratulated her on the bravery and leadership she had shown in the fight for civil liberties. While slightly more retiring, I had engaged in a heated televised debate with the county prosecutor and the chief narcotics officer for the region. The debate room was packed with people. A local defense attorney and I challenged the policies and practices of the prosecutor and his top narcotics officer. The video tape of the debate was played again and again on our (desperate for material) public access television station and the prosecutor was reported to be complaining that he had been bushwhacked.

With further abuses and broadening community activism, the controversial young narcotics officer left for a different job and the county commissioners held their vote to refuse further money. The politics had been hot, heavy, and bitter. They are angrier and more personal in this small town of real people and close contacts. Though we lived out in the rural regions of the county, we had been at the center of the battle. And now, as we sat five hundred miles away, our opponents were searching our farm and home, with no one there to witness or represent us, attempting to build a case that we were responsible for the large growing operation they had discovered in the federal forest that adjoins our land. Compounding the fear was uncertainty—while we were vacationing, our home-under-construction was in the hands of house-sitters, carpenters, and masons. For all we knew, there could be a neutron bomb on the dining room table. On the day after the search, close friends go to the house (the house-sitters had, understandably, tendered their resignations). They followed the trail of the sheriff's vehicles and found a patch of green stumps surrounded by remnants of a green deer fence made out of some sort of nylon cord. Back at the house, they went through the search warrant and related documents. We learned that the "inventory" of items seized from the house and outbuildings during the search showed a mix of items including "101 marihuana plants," a flowered bag with twine, a "photograph with a marijuana leaf," cigarette papers, and wire with green twine. On these points, we confronted all forms of midnight fears. Had sections of twine matching the deer fence been planted in the shed? Had one of the people with access to the shed used our twine to make the fence? Were twine, a photograph, and cigarette papers enough evidence to indict us?

A few small points of information had been gathered from the hodgepodge of two heavily trafficked buildings and a nearby national forest and made into an official statement about us. We could not edit it or control it and we had no clear knowledge about its implications. I came to understand more and more about the experience of the welfare mothers as they try to live in a world in which unknown people put together small bits of information, organize them according to unknown hunches, rules, and guidelines, and decide whether or not to construct a story that leaves the subject untouched or sends them to jail.

Am I innocent? Yes. Angry? Yes. Terrified to the core of my existence? Yes.

A diamond-shaped region of locked muscular fear extends from my navel up and out to my shoulders, then up to my throat and on through to what feels to be the inside of my skull. Wave after wave of near cramping and roaring through the entire region. The mind runs mad with uncontrollable ideas. I flee to a worst-case scenario— planted evidence, an indictment, a humiliating public trial, conviction. Handcuffs. Loss of my tenured professorship. Forfeiture of the farm. Prison. My family scattered. And then, later, trying to feed and clothe my children with few skills, a criminal record, and a broken career. I picture us, in the end, stripped of our careers and our home.

We struggle to hold on to a small apartment or trailer. Amy waits tables. I do odd carpentry and deliver pizza in an effort to make the rent. My kids have no insurance, my glasses are taped at the hinges because I can't afford to repair them, and the moss green wall-to-wall carpet is sticky with grime.

It wasn't until much later that I could recognize that the imaginary hell to which I was sending myself was close to the daily lives of several of the people I had been studying for this book. That my hell could be the daily life of someone I purported to represent in my writing drives home the enormity of the unbridgeable gaps in class, context, and experience. And the differences in our responses and our resources became even more apparent as events unfolded. Within several minutes of having received news of the investigation, we contacted a friend who was a defense attorney specializing in police misconduct and search and seizure law. We told him what had happened and what we had learned about the day's events. *Did they find any pot on your land?* No. *Did they find any pot in the house?* No. *Did they find any fifty-gallon drums of Miracle Gro?* No. *Calm down,* he said, *In these cases they have to "catch you in the patch" to make any charges stick. This wouldn't even go beyond an investigation most places, but, then again, we live in a weird place.*

With that comment went all the comfort of the "Calm down" and we once again settled into a cycle that moved from anger, to fear, to sadness, but allowed no break from a maddening intensity of emotional force. Little sleep and no food. Though I came nowhere close to a serious thought of it, I came to know that an accused man, though innocent, could take his own life simply to escape the unbearable roaring of existence.

We were away for three more days before the eight-hour drive home. Our hosts did their best to reassure us and we did our best to keep the kids on vacation. We edged toward exhaustion as we loaded the car to go back and face whatever was coming. At that point, neither we nor our attorney knew whether we faced immediate arrest in front of our children, a midnight visit by the sheriff's department, or front-page coverage in the local paper. When none of that happened and we were told that it would probably not—at least for a while— we settled into a slightly less panicked state of existence. We took photographs and worked to clean up the house. We exclaimed over the mess in the kids' rooms and the rifled boxes of family photographs. We went up to the site, took pictures and videos, and began recording the many abuses and oversights that had occurred.

THE SEARCH

We know only a few things about what happened while the police were visiting. According to our house-sitter, it was around two o'clock when she noticed that a black helicopter was circling over the large forested area that lies behind our farm. Minutes later she was startled to hear the helicopter land in one of our upper fields, and moments after that even more surprised to see several cars and trucks come across the small private bridge which crosses a creek to come onto our land. The vehicles came up the four-hundred-foot gravel driveway and parked next to the house. A squad of deputies and agents— led by the sheriff himself—began unloading small all-terrain vehicles (ATVs) in the gravel-and-grass area next to our house and gardens.

Before attempting to get a search warrant, the agents got on their ATVs and took off through the small lane that cuts through our gardens, beside our two outbuildings, and past the large swing set that I had built for the children. They began climbing the steep windy trails to travel the quarter mile back to the area where the helicopter had apparently landed. Next, our visitors waded through tall brush and grasses to a navel-high six-strand barbed wire fence. This was our heavily posted property line and beyond it lay some two hundred acres of National Forest as well as hundreds of more acres of privately owned forest land. They climbed over the fence to hike another two hundred feet into the forest, traveling through heavy undergrowth, over rough but flat terrain, and then onto a mild slope that faces away from our land. There, in two separate plots, roughly a third of a mile from our home, was a garden of what is said to be about a hundred plants. (In the affidavit requesting a search warrant for our home, the sheriff's investigator made no mention of the third-of-a-mile hike from our house or the fact that the marijuana was not on our land.)

As we studied and photographed the area, it became harder and harder to see how the sheriff could have made a reasonable case for searching our house. There are two semi-abandoned roads traversing the area in which the pot was growing. One would let you drive a passenger car from a public road to within 175 yards of the marijuana plants. There, a well-worn footpath connected the gardens and the roadway. There were also numerous game trails from our massive population of white-tailed deer. Because of all these trails, the section of National Forest that the plants were found in is regularly used by hikers, hunters, horseback riders, and four-wheeler enthusiasts. One day a few years back, two tall and rather distinguished looking hikers came out of the woods while I was gardening. They said that they had gotten lost as they walked around to break in some new boots before a major hiking trip out west. We chatted amiably in the garden for a few minutes; I offered them water and a lift, but they declined and went off down the road to find their car. I suppose I could have jumped on them for trespassing across my well-marked property, but it seemed like an idea that was both grumpy and unwise. The lead hiker, you see, was the judge of the County Court of Common Pleas and the very man who would later sign the warrant to invade our home.

Prior to searching our house, the deputies had figured out that the plants were not on our land. Our house-sitter overheard this at 5:30. Clearly there had been a mistake. Perhaps the search warrant should be modified or reconsidered. But no. The doors of our home were opened and our dressers, beds, desks, toy closets, jewelry and medicine cabinets were all thrown open to the pawing hands of the deputies. Letters, family photos, underwear, jewelry, even our children's toys were tossed, dumped, and rifled. I hope that the reader can pause and imagine absolutely every nook and cranny of your home ransacked not just by strangers, but by strangers who would probably like nothing more than to hang you out to dry.

Trying to Live

A good indication of how stressed out I was by all of this is that it was not until fully a week later that I made a connection between these events and the work that waited on the desk and computer in my office. At the time that the helicopter, ATVs, and agents were visiting our farm, I was just about finished writing a book about the ways that people speak, think, and struggle with the impact of surveillance in their lives. My loss of awareness regarding the idea of *surveillance* goes a long way toward showing how an abstract conceptualization such as this becomes less meaningful in the lived context of chase, struggle, and fear. When we talk about things like "surveillance" or "privacy" or "rights" we artificially reify and distinguish particular elements or feelings out of broad and complex processes of political and social action. Just as the women we interviewed so often seemed to blur need, frustration, hope, caseworkers, men, computers, neighbors, children, rules, and other things into a flowing montage of life on welfare, we were experiencing a blur of helicopters, lawyers, police, children, money, neighbors, fear, and all the other mundane things like housecleaning, cooking, and getting in the winter's wood supply. It is not that we "blurred" these things, but that academic analysis—my own included—so often *deblurs* the lived world as it abstracts particular and constructed elements of situations.

Close to the end of writing this book I had been frustrated by hitting the wall that every ethnographer or social observer confronts— we can't *really* know how the people we study feel. Despite dozens of readings and listenings to tapes and transcripts, I knew that I could never fully understand the feelings and responses that these parents went through as they tried to care for their children and protect their families within a context of permanent investigation. Now, although there is of course a remaining gap created by differences in class, gender, and experience, I feel a hell of a lot closer.

I feel a self-awareness that I would have previously called paranoia. I wonder late at night about what some faceless bureaucrat in the law enforcement agencies is thinking and doing about "my case." There is a constant and fully physical sense of fear and insecurity as I know that with a few more turns of either bad luck or malfeasance on the part of my enemies all that I had built up would be gone. And I knew, fully, that they *were* my enemies and that my way of life was profoundly threatened. I knew some of these men only well enough to distrust them and dislike them and they the same toward me. But I was also uncertain. Maybe there was no prejudice, maybe it was all just a series of accidents and coincidences that led the helicopters and deputies to our farm and home. Who can know, other than the men themselves? (And, in some ways, the sound possibility that this was a chance search and not a targeted shakedown is even more troubling, for it means that any home within the general vicinity of marijuana plants is subject to a full search. For rural families in the nation's numerous marijuana growing areas, any protection that could be offered by the Fourth Amendment is effectively destroyed.)

The personal living of these understandings went far, I think, toward helping me understand how the subjects of a surveillance regime must feel. I had listened to the women we interviewed describe their feelings with such words as "awful" or "a nightmare"—but I never gave the terms the sort of stomach churning credit that they really deserved. Beyond that new understanding though, the differences in our situations are stark and immediate. The welfare mothers we had interviewed said almost nothing about ideas like privacy, rights, or the power of the law to help them. We had called a defense attorney within minutes of hearing the news; hired a former judge as our attorney within a few days; and consulted with the state director of the ACLU and a widely recognized civil rights attorney in subsequent weeks. The welfare mothers were able to learn relatively little about the complex bureaucratic processes that defined their condition; our attorney explained it and promised—for a thousand-dollar retainer and $150 an hour—to guide us through it. And although we shared with them all the ineffable, unprintable, personal, parental, and physical rage about what was done to us, we also were able to state our frustrations in legal terms—due process, warrants, the Fourth Amendment—which eluded them in both life and doctrine. And we were able to turn to forms of legal action—attorneys, evidence gathering, documentation—designed to protect us from the assault. Were we using "rights talk"? All the time.

But there was also a lot of care talk going on. What would be the impact of arrest or litigation on our children? How would we provide for them in a worst-case scenario? How were they coping with the stress that pervaded our household? (Poorly enough that after the first week we decided to create a zone of silence about everything related to the search.) In short, every calculation and decision that we attempted to make about how we were going to cope with the law was embedded in a context of thinking about our own needs for money, security, and dignity and our children's needs for a sane household, nonincarcerated parents, and, of course, all the money we might need to spend on litigation.

Into the second week, we settle into a routine—appetites are back and sleep comes more easily. This is in part because we have much more information about what took place, what rules of warrants and evidence exist, and how weak and flawed a case the police would have if they attempted to move against us. We have also had the reassurances of many wonderful friends and community members who understand our anger, our fears, and the true potential for political paybacks from the sheriff and the prosecutor's office. But I think part of the routine must be a numbing as well, and I am coming to understand how the welfare mothers I am studying are able to live their lives. Simply put, it would be psychologically and physically impossible to maintain and attend to the level of stress and fear that had dominated our lives in week one. One must adjust or snap. Since the situation cannot be changed, in the short run anyway, the heart and mind must. There are still moments. Trying to eat at our backyard picnic table is hard with the tracks of the ATV in the dirt three feet away. The barking of our dogs, the sound of a slowing vehicle, or the thump of tires on our old wooden bridge jerks our heads to the windows to see if a sheriff's car is coming up the driveway. Lying in our bedroom we can feel the residue of the invasion.

I think that we must create illusions of autonomy and security. Living far from town, on a gravel road sided by fields and forests, we were probably about as close to isolation as one could be and still work at a major university. But the illusions of security don't hold up very well under assaults like this, and I doubt that they will ever have as much clout in the future. Perhaps that is part of the power of surveillance—to remind us, to notify us, to keep us on our toes because even if they are not watching right now, they might be soon.

Invasions beyond Privacy

As this manuscript is completed, there has been no ending to this story. The sheriff's department has never contacted us. A federal agent called once, but never again. Helicopters have been back to spend thirty minutes hovering over our house and land. Some of our neighbors have heard rumors that cause them to keep their children away from ours. Another needs to ask us if we are drug dealers before she will allow her daughter to babysit. As for the cops, they may prosecute us, we may sue them. It may all just disappear quietly in the annals of this work, our hearts, and the law enforcement filing systems. Whatever happens, we will never again be able to return to the sense of security and isolation that marked a small farm far from town. Even though the police search turned up no new or valuable information, it sent a message—a message that we are never really alone and that the powers of the state to demand and enforce compliance are, as it looks now, almost unlimited.

The invasion of our home was a massive violation of our privacy. But, quite frankly, that part of the politics of surveillance was among the most fleeting. What continued was how the structures of power, surveillance, and law interacted with the realities of our daily lives to rob us of what we felt to be both our integrity and our citizenship. As we spoke with friends late one night a few months after the search, we went through our options. We could sue. Two attorneys were interested. But the costs seemed high. Money, exposure, stress on us and the children, time spent hassling with lawyers and bureaucrats instead of family, work, music, livestock, and gardens. And, of course, the possibility that poking the authorities with a lawsuit would provoke retaliatory action. We all knew that a small amount of planted evidence, a hostile prosecutor, and an angry sheriff could do a lot of damage to our lives. And we all knew enough about local law enforcement to know that such concerns were not even mildly far-fetched. In this way, then, all the accessibility that we had felt regarding the language of rights was misleading. We could speak them, but we could not really afford them.

As an alternative to litigation, we could use our experience as an example. By sharing it with others through speaking and writing, we could perhaps call more attention to the problems of police abuse and government surveillance. But this, too, involved risks of retaliation, expense, and, ironically, continued invasions of our privacy. We could, finally, "lump it." Call it a learning experience, try to forget about it, and move on. No more money spent. No more stress on the kids. A

reduced chance of "paybacks" through planted evidence or harass-
ment. But, of course, a massively diminished sense of integrity, autonomy, and citizenship.

So what, in the end, was the invasion? It *was* a violation of privacy
but it was much, much more. Like so many of the welfare mothers
that we had interviewed, the most profound violation is of our capacity to "do the right thing." Following the stern advice of our attorney, we have quieted our activism and said little about what happened or anything else related to our local constabulary. Our friends
have been asked to silence themselves and anyone who speaks about
these events. The combined impact of the state's power to compel,
watch, and punish, the sheriff's power to retaliate against challenge,
and our duty to meet the needs of our family, has stolen the senses of
autonomy and control upon which full citizenship is based. In the
end, though much separates us from women like Mary, Delilah, and
the others, we have a shared condition as subjects of a surveillance society. We are all watched, we are all angry, and we are all afraid. And
we are increasingly without a language to speak about it.

APPENDIX:

FORMAT FOR SEMI-STRUCTURED

INTERVIEW

NOTE: This is meant to be a guideline not an exact script. Make sure you avoid cuing the interviewee about law, privacy, or rights; but other than that feel free to use wordings that are most comfortable to you.

CONSENT FORM: Tell them what's up, explain the form, have them sign it before beginning.

DEMOGRAPHICS: Age range, family size, time spent on welfare, types of programs used, county of residence.

ICEBREAKER: Why did you go on welfare? *(Try to get the story)*

•

When you first applied for assistance, how did you feel about the welfare office's requests for documentation of rent, utilities, birth certificates, and Social Security Cards?

Why do you think the welfare office wants so much information and documentation?

Do you think the welfare agency would be able to find out if you did not report that you took a job in another county? Or had savings in a bank in another state? Or received unemployment or disability payments? *(How or why not for each.)*

Have you, yourself, ever kept things from your caseworker or bent the truth about income, family size, or work history in order to improve your benefits? Any unreported cash income?

If not, why not?

If so, did you get caught?

What about other folks you know, what sorts of things do people do to make ends meet?

How do you feel about people who don't fully report their income or resources? *(Why?)*

Do you talk with other welfare clients and share information about rules, caseworkers, or different programs? Did you ever get or give any advice on how to apply for programs or report information?

A few years ago, the welfare system started using a new statewide computer called CRIS-E. In general, has your service and delivery of benefits gotten better or worse with the new computer? *(For post-computer clients, simply ask how their service has been with the new computer.)* (How? Examples? How else? Any complaints?)

Can you tell me what sorts of information the computer has about you and your family? *(Fully probe awareness of their own data file, number matching and other types of verification; don't cue them at this point; just use vague questions.)* What else? What else? What else?

We've talked a fair bit about how computers have changed the way welfare works, but I now want to give you some more information about the new system. The welfare office is able to do what are called computer number matches, where they use the Social Security numbers of people in your family to look and see if you have money or income that you're not reporting. They use information from state and federal taxes, Social Security information, statewide wage records, and information from unemployment compensation, workman's comp., and state retirement systems. They make a computer check of this information several times a year and your caseworker gets all of this information.

Were you aware of this?

How do you feel about it? *(Push them to talk and explain.)*

Have you ever gotten any letters or had to see your caseworker because of something that turned up in a wage match or some other way? (If so, what happened, how was it resolved?)

Do you think it will prevent fraud and cheating?

How do you think people will work around it?

Does it bother you when they do so much checking up on you? Why or why not? *(Push them to talk and explain.)*

In some states, the welfare agency fingerprints their clients to make sure they are who they say they are. How do you feel about that? Why?

•

Debrief: Has this interview raised any questions that you would like to ask me, or made you think of things that you would like to bring up?

•

If you are left with any questions or concerns, you may want to talk with your caseworker or their supervisor, or you may want to consult with legal services, which can provide you with free legal advice about problems or questions you have about your benefits. *(Provide phone numbers for local offices.)*

NOTES

INTRODUCTION

1. The prevailing framework for most legislation and regulation is the "data protection" or "privacy protection" model that emerged under the Fair Information Principles of the early 1970s. Ample scholarship suggests that the model is inadequate for newer technologies of surveillance and probably didn't work all that well to begin with (see Bennett and Grant 1999; Marx 1999, 41–43). Recent works on surveillance and privacy include a melange of proposals for new approaches, including but not limited to commodification models, the further development of rights, self-protective technologies, privacy commissioner systems, and mass protest. There is an increasingly shared sense that the conventional framework is in need of some sort of repair or expansion (Regan 1995). Amid all the debate, surprisingly little attention is paid to asking the subjects of intensive surveillance what they think (see, however, Gandy 1993). The outstanding collections of essays in Bennett and Grant 1999, and the more technically oriented symposium in Agre and Rotenberg 1997 provide a thorough introduction to these concerns.

2. We also spoke with numerous welfare administrators and caseworkers about their perspectives; while these insights are used to fill out our picture of the welfare surveillance system, the main focus of this work, by far, is on the clients themselves.

3. This will hardly be a real surprise to readers more familiar with recent research on rights claiming and legal consciousness. As discussed later in this work, Engel and Munger (1996), for example, found little explicit rights claiming even when research subjects were explicitly covered by formal legal protections such as the Americans with Disabilities Act. Kristin Bumiller's research among victims of discrimination found a similar rights reticence (1988). Rights claiming, it would appear, is not as automatic and widespread as authors such as Glendon assert (1991). The present project hopes to contribute to the ongoing research by exploring the social conditions of rights reticence and, more centrally, the types of language and action that take place when rights are not at hand.

4. As discussed later in this work, the dichotomization of "rights" and "care" used here is admittedly too simple to convey the actual practices and

potentials. In the seemingly endless malleability and creativity of languages and politics, when we speak of things like a "discourse of rights" and a "discourse of care" we are constructing temporary heuristics that can help us talk about a very messy and shifting world. Noting this, it is also important to remember that heuristics, and forms of claiming, can be powerful stuff. As discussed later, Bussiere (1997) argues that an important factor in the breakup of the National Welfare Rights Organization (NWRO) was a battle between male attorneys, who pushed a strategy of universalized rights, and the poor women membership, who preferred a stronger recognition of their unique status as mothers with small children (100–101).

5. The "language of rights" covers a good deal. Animal rights, rights to equal treatment, property rights, right to life, voting rights, and a multitude of other claims fall under this broad umbrella, and many rights claims clearly challenge ideas of individualism and abstraction. I should emphasize that this work centers on a particular and unique right: the right to privacy, the right to be let alone, which, I would argue, is outstanding—along with the closely related right to private property—in its individualism and its tendency to abstract (see Regan 1995). Even here, though, we will want to note that seemingly individualistic rights claims can help to build community, relationships, and participation by creating needed boundaries, protections for interactions, and the recognition of shared values (Engel and Munger 1996; Waldron 1996).

6. For at least the last generation, activism around the idea of privacy has been a blue-ribbon arena of specialists, lawyers, and corporate leaders. Privacy activist Simon Davies notes that the debate over surveillance was both broader and more robust in the 1960s and early 1970s, particularly in Europe, but that, "Since the late 1970[s] the environment of privacy activism changed substantially. Privacy protection in more recent years has been widely perceived as constituting a set of technical rules governing the handling of data. A scan of privacy-related publications in the two decades from 1970 indicates a steady decrease in polemical works and a corresponding increase in technical and legal works" (1999, 245). Privacy politics, he continues, went "mainstream" as activists and organizations "came to depend on institutional funding, particularly from philanthropic trusts and companies. Increasingly, as the issues became more sophisticated, representatives from commerce and government were invited to join the movement" (ibid.).

7. I will not be arguing that these different ways of speaking are irreconcilable, exclusive, or linked to immutable characteristics (see Waldron 1996). Nor do I want to suggest that one is in some universal sense "superior" to the other (ibid.). This is a story about a particular time and place and how things make sense within that context.

8. This rights reticence may only be tied to the surveillance policies and bureaucratic policing of welfare policy—if it came to things like divorce, free speech, or other areas, it could be that the turn to rights would be more apparent.

CHAPTER ONE

1. "Application for Income, Medical, and Food Assistance," Ohio Department of Human Services, Form 7100 (Rev. 9/87), p. 31.

2. "Most officials and reformers would have agreed that any relief given to the able-bodied should be as unpleasant and degrading as possible. . . . Only those men willing to break stone or cut wood for their meager supper and spartan bed should be sheltered from the streets" (Katz 1986, 92).

3. "Scientific charity was not only a set of principles that guided action; it also was a method for gathering data with which to further develop the law of charity and reform. Charity organizations, their leaders felt, should study as well as help the poor. In New York, the Charity Organization Society meticulously classified its cases and mapped their distribution by streets and even houses" (ibid., 69).

4. "When the Social Security Act was passed, only ADC required that clients be 'needy.' To establish need a client had to be not only without income but also without resources, including property or services which many at the time considered essential, such as telephones or automobiles or houses, and which might stave off poverty and help a temporarily reduced client regain position. Cash savings were not allowed. Thus in many instances an ADC applicant would have to get rid of useful resources even at a loss, impoverishing herself in order to qualify. . . . By contrast one could have millions and still collect unemployment compensation or OAI (Old Age Insurance)" (Gordon 1994, 297).

5. Enforcement of these rules included inspections of the home and "midnight raids" by welfare agents trying to uncover evidence of a "man in the house": "The object of the raid is to discover a 'man in the house' or 'substitute parent,' whose presence, depending on the jurisdiction, either precludes giving assistance altogether or gives rise to an inference of support, which, of course, the public assistance agency is obligated to investigate and to take into account in determining the unmet budgetary need" (Handler and Rosenheim, 1966, 282–382). Man-in-the-house rules were deemed unconstitutional by the U.S. Supreme Court in *King v. Smith* 329 U.S. 309 1968; see Trattner 1999, 310.

6. In "Privacy in Welfare," Joel Handler and Margaret Rosenheim summarized the state of AFDC surveillance: "[B]y the nature of public assistance, the task of determining eligibility is never-ending. Unlike the duty to pay income taxes, which calls for calculating taxable income accumulated over a prescribed period of time, the obligation of the recipient to report changes in status that alter his needs or his income or resources is continuing. For administrative purposes, enforcement of this obligation is discharged through periodic checks by welfare authorities, but the recipient carries the burden of reporting when his circumstances change, else he is liable to penalties including prosecution for fraud, permanent or temporary termination of his grant, or withholding from future grants the excess deemed to have been paid out in the past. Having satisfied the authority of his initial eligibility the client must regularly submit to a truncated version of the same process.

Furthermore, because of the requirement to report changed circumstances he can be requested to furnish explanations of inconsistencies in his own statements or of the allegations of third parties that bear upon his eligibility. 'Failure to comply' suffices to close a case" (1966, 382).

7. As Blanche Bernstein, then Deputy Commissioner for Income Maintenance from New York, testified in 1977: "from about the early 1960s until about 1971, the administration of welfare in New York City was, indeed, a rather loose affair. It was the days of the self-declaration and the self-recertification, of separation of services, of an era in which . . . no one worker in the system knew anything about any particular family" (House Committee on Government Operations, subcommittee hearings, *Administration of the AFDC Program*, 95th Cong., 1st sess., 1977, 161).

8. Critics of the declaration process argued that it allowed impermissibly high levels of fraud and error in AFDC administration, but others disagreed. Complaining about the extensive regulations and verification procedures that had been put in place by the mid-1970s, Leon Ginsberg, commissioner of the West Virginia Department of Welfare, testified before Congress that "my statisticians tell me that there was no significant difference in error rates under the simplified declaration system and the rather tedious interviews, home visits, and complex eligibility determination we perform now" (ibid., 367).

9. Governors Rockefeller (N.Y.) and Reagan (Cal.)—whose states had over half of the nation's welfare clients—began large-scale campaigns against fraud, and other states followed suit. In Nevada, the welfare agency responded "by mobilizing virtually the entire work force of the department to interview employers and neighbors of the poor and to study the records of the social security and unemployment compensation agencies for any evidence of unreported income in the preceding five or more years." When nearly half of Nevada's welfare recipients saw their benefits terminated or reduced without notice or consultation, the National Welfare Rights Organization mobilized "some forty lawyers and seventy law students" and held mass demonstrations. "On March 20 the Federal District Court issued an order reinstating everyone who had been terminated or who had received reduced grants, and retroactive payments were ordered" (Piven and Cloward 1979, 333).

10. One man, the father of a teenaged child he never knew of, conceived during group sex involving a woman who could not recall his name, was reportedly located in a prison several states away (author's interview).

11. IEVS was required in the Deficit Reduction Act of 1984 (PL 98-369) after being advocated by the Grace Commission; see Reichman 1987, 399.

12. Perhaps the most important feature of CRIS-E in relation to the caseworkers has to do with the processing of eligibility interviews. Previously, caseworker and client would work together filling out "the book"—a thirty-some-page application document. With CRIS-E, however, caseworkers no longer face the client, they face the screen. And they no longer fill out the book, they type in information requested by the many "screens" of "the drivers": CRIS-E's automatic, self-propelled format for client interviews. As one caseworker phrased it: "you just follow the screens . . . and run through the

drivers" or, another: "the driver just takes you one screen and the next and everything seems evident."

The driver displaces the caseworker as the one in charge of the interview. In fact, several spoke in great frustration about how "the driver" made them go through redundant screens or ask clients obviously irrelevant questions—sometimes making a small change could take up to an hour of time—and there is by design no way for the caseworker to override the driver in these situations. So they clearly lose control and almost seem to serve as assistants to CRIS-E in the interviewing process.

One very important result of this change is that caseworkers are no longer required to be completely familiar with the rules and regulations regarding the administration of the various programs: "I came in as a caseworker with the [computer] system. I had to read the manual but a lot of that stuff doesn't stick with me and the computer figures all of this up. . . . Before the system, caseworkers had to know exactly . . . I should [know], but it's not something I have to keep remembering because the system's going to do it for me."

In another interview with two seasoned caseworkers, the lack of independent knowledge on the part of new caseworkers was highlighted as an important issue. "CRIS-E makes a lot of mistakes and caseworkers make a lot of errors as far as data input. . . . [Another caseworker] and I have been at it long enough that when CRIS-E pops out something at the end that doesn't look right bells go off and we've . . . been in CRIS-E so much we know which screens to go back to, to figure out what went wrong. And to make the change and to make it work right. New caseworkers come on; they don't have a clue, they're totally lost in space and they don't know what codes to use, they don't know where to find the codes, they wouldn't know what to do with the codes if they had 'em."

13. As David Dery argued in 1981, aptly describing the pre-CRIS-E situation in states like Ohio, "Welfare is usually characterized by its complexity: a multitude of programs that originates in three levels of government, a multitude of eligibility standards for different programs, and a multitude of vague and constantly changing regulations. . . . Whereas county administration of welfare is meant to make a complex enterprise manageable, it also means only a loose supervision by the state over what the counties do with state and federal money. . . . The promise of a statewide information system is that it should be followed by increased rationality, better decision making, supervision, evaluation, and analysis" (16–19).

14. So, for example, if an applicant has a savings account in Oregon, the caseworker in rural Ohio will come into work one morning and find an "alert" on their screen. When the alert is called up, it will show that a computer sweep of the Internal Revenue Service 1099 interest and dividend data shows that the client is earning enough interest in Oregon to indicate a significant savings account. The client is then contacted to account for the situation and the caseworker, as well as the county's fraud control officer, work to decide what appropriate actions and charges are. (The client will never be told the source of the information, since the IRS insists that its role in the process be secret.)

15. One unintended side effect is that with so many small cases of over-payment being detected, each of which requires slow repayment by impov-erished people, one county agency has nearly as many repayment accounts as it does active cases.

16. Prior to the computerization of welfare surveillance, caseworkers and fraud control officers had few options. They relied almost solely on the "rat call"—a tip from a neighbor or angry relative of a cheater. As Billy G. Davis, head of the National Association of State Welfare Fraud Directors put it: "Nothing was happening before computer matching." Due to limits on the surveillance capacity of the state—the gaps or blind spots in its vision—a wide range of income-enhancing or survival efforts were possible. Individuals could feasibly receive assistance benefits while receiving income from a job, worker's compensation, retirement benefits, assistance in a neighboring state, or other sources. But the new surveillance capacity manifest in the comput-erization of fraud control closes many of the gaps and, in turn, many of the opportunities for beating the system. Multi-state and federal computer files covering employment, unemployment compensation, retirement, Social Se-curity, savings and investments, and other recorded holdings are cross-checked on a regular basis, thereby dramatically reducing possibilities for re-sisting the rules and prohibitions of the welfare system.

17. Although Scott here writes about a different and more epochal his-torical transformation, his words ring true for these changes in the imple-mentation of welfare surveillance and the extent to which the state is no longer sightless: "The premodern state was, in many crucial respects, par-tially blind; it knew precious little about its subjects, their wealth, their land-holdings and yields, their location, their very identity. It lacked anything like a detailed 'map' of its terrain and its people. It lacked for the most part, a measure, a metric, that would allow it to 'translate' what it knew into a com-mon standard necessary for a synoptic view" (Scott 1998, 2).

CHAPTER TWO

1. AFDC was a federally supported program administered by the states, so there can be a great deal of variation between states. Since this study is based in the state of Ohio, aspects of its story may be specific to that state's programs. On the other hand, nearly every state was under significant pres-sure from the federal government to enhance and upgrade their surveillance capacity during the 1980s, and there was much sharing and cross-fertilization in the design of programs. So, while specific programs vary from state to state, the programs here nonetheless provide a sound insight as to the general tenor of welfare surveillance. With the 1996 replacement of AFDC by Temporary Assistance to Needy Families (TANF), many aspects of "welfare" changed, but the surveillance capacities studied here remain largely the same.

2. Interviews with frontline welfare caseworkers, though, indicate that many use small informal ways of assisting some of their clients to maximize program benefits. This can range from subtle cuing about how to answer a question regarding food stamp use to outright falsification of children's ages in order to sidestep what is perceived as a "ridiculous" rule.

3. Further, the ways of knowing that traditional survey methods produce —simple responses to predefined categories and questions—are precisely the ways of knowing that mark the bureaucratic system of surveillance that we hoped to learn about. As explained earlier, one way to learn about the powers and effects of bureaucratic surveillance is to study the same social terrain with a markedly different, or even oppositional perspective. Clearly, a quick precoded survey instrument was inappropriate.

4. See Appendix for the interview guide sheet. Early in the process, the interviewers removed a few of the draft questions as inappropriate or "stupid" and added several which they felt were essential to drawing out a full account.

5. Four of the original interviews were largely unusable due to recording errors or background noise.

6. The consent forms bore what the subjects presented as their true names, but were never associated with the tapes or transcripts and have since been destroyed.

7. I use the term "we" frequently throughout the work. Although I did not personally undertake the interviews with clients, I did participate extensively in the development of the guidelines and, obviously, the interpretation of the results. And although the other participants in the project did not undertake interviews with administrators and caseworkers (I did those), they helped, in different ways, to frame my questions and my understandings. So many aspects of the primary research stem from a collaboration of people that the "we" seems to be the best pronoun to use.

Although the question about "getting by" does not appear in the final guidesheet, in practice it came up as a natural opening in the interviews.

8. One reason for silence on the reason of the inspection may be that many number matches are considered confidential—even to the people whom they report on. For example, within IEVS is a number match utilizing Internal Revenue Service data. Traditionally, IRS data has not been used for law enforcement and the agency is apparently sensitive about this program. Therefore, as I was told in confidential interviews with welfare administrators, the existence of the IRS number matches is kept as confidential information.

9. It is probably an inescapable problem of this sort of research and writing that the loquacious get more print and, therefore, seem to define the group as a whole. There were only one or two interviews in which answers were so brief and cryptic as to be close to unusable, a fortunate outcome which may be tied to the methodological approach laid out at the beginning of chapter 2.

10. Rebecca: "If I was in the right frame of mind you would write a book about my life. It wouldn't just be about being on welfare, it would be about meeting the wrong person and domestic violence and living in poverty and living in a dump and I just think there is a lot more problems to be concerned about."

11. Research such as this may be trapped by "state ways of seeing." Even, and perhaps especially, in an effort to critically challenge the state's view of

the "welfare poor," this work accepts that class of people as the focus and therefore seems cursed to replicate some facets of the bureaucratic forms of knowledge. To combat this, as explained in the section on methodology, every effort has been made to "see" them in ways that combat the state's ways of seeing. Works such as Ewick and Silbey 1998, Yngvesson 1993, and Merry 1990 explore issues of law and conflict in more diverse populations.

12. Because of the transiency of welfare status, there are a few cases in which the women had been receiving AFDC until shortly before the interview or were in the process of going off at the time that we spoke.

13. This point relates to the overall epistemology of this project. The sort of categorizing, codified ways of knowing that are produced when content analysis programs are applied to interviews such as this replicate the forms of knowing that can mark advanced surveillance systems. They force the diverse and messy into neat grids; clearing the underbrush to create an overview. Some simplification and concentration is unavoidable in any attempt to make sense of the world, but in the project at hand, we try to maintain a strong commitment to local claims and understandings, contextual meanings, and an appreciation for the messiness of everyday political discourse.

14. Even with all the secret stories that we heard, everyone involved in the research project was convinced that there were more that could be told; that our methods and approach were helping us get to a lot of what was going on, but that no one could ever get it all.

CHAPTER THREE

1. See *Rights at Work* (McCann 1994); "Legal Mobilization: The Neglected Role of Law in the Political System" (Zemans 1983); *Poor People's Movements* (Piven and Cloward 1979); and *The Politics of Rights* (Scheingold 1974).

2. As Austin Sarat has argued: "The law that the welfare poor confront is neither a law of reason and justification nor of sacred texts and shared commitments. [They] are not invited to participate in the interpretation of those texts, and they are included in neither the official explication of welfare law nor in the construction of meaningful accounts of the legal practices they regularly encounter. They are 'caught' inside law's rules, but are, at the same time, excluded from its interpretive community" (1990, 345–346).

3. An adequate review of the history of the welfare rights movement is beyond the scope and mission of this work. See the outstanding accounts by Elizabeth Bussiere (1997) and Martha Davis (1993).

4. Clearly, as an extensive body of research has shown (see, among others, Scheingold 1974; McCann 1994; Epp 1998), the missing factors of activist lawyers and leaders are important pieces of the puzzle. Yet given our special interest in popular consciousness—how lay people speak and think about surveillance—the pages that follow devote most of their attention to the condition and status of the poor themselves.

5. Perhaps part of the reason that more persistent rights claims do not develop in this population is related to their transience—few people experi-

ence welfare as a long-term situation and fewer still think that they will be on for much longer than they have been. See Handler 1973, 148–149.

6. The "spontaneity" McCann refers to is confined to the interviews themselves—in no sense would he depict the broader mobilization of rights as "spontaneous." Rather, *Rights at Work* (1994) emphasizes the interaction of courts, activists, and broader political coalitions in the process of legal mobilization.

7. Although Sarat (1990) found more evidence of the use of law as a tactical resource in the hands of the welfare poor, it should be noted that since his interviewees were initially contacted in the waiting room of the Legal Services office, the sample was predisposed toward legal action.

8. See, for example, *Greater Cleveland Welfare Rights Organization et al. v. Bauer et al.*, 462 F. Supp. 1313 (United States District Court, Northern District of Ohio, Eastern Div. 1978), and *Fifteen Thousand Eight Hundred and Forty-four Welfare Recipients v. King et al.*, 610 F. 2d 32 (United States Court of Appeals 1st Cir. 1979).

9. "[A]ctivists appropriated the language of rights to interpret, or 'name,' a long-experienced injustice in new, more compelling and sensible terms. In this way, the inchoate legal consciousness shared by many similarly situated citizens was collectively tapped, expanded, and focused on specific demands for change. Bound by mutual perceptions of right and seemingly supported by the courts, potential movement activists suddenly found themselves in a more propitious relationship to established power" (McCann 1994, 89).

10. A number of recent works raise substantial doubt about whether the poor ever view their situation as "legitimate" or accept the "authority" of their rulers. See, in particular, Sarat 1990; Scott 1985.

11. Let me here emphasize a point that is made clear in the following chapter: I am not arguing that these women are without power—for it is clear that they can and do undertake many actions to advance their situation. Nor am I suggesting that they are without "legal consciousness"—they are profoundly and overwhelmingly defined by law and their awareness of it and their transgressions of it—but they do seem to make little use of the subset of legal consciousness that speaks to the ennobling and liberatory capacity of "rights."

12. As Edin found in her study of Chicago welfare mothers: "AFDC budgets are almost always set at levels on which nobody could possibly live. No one involved in the system had a plausible story about how anyone could pay for even basic needs on such a budget. Yet it is, in theory, almost impossible to supplement such a budget with outside income. The obvious question is 'What's going on?' . . . *All fifty of the Chicago welfare recipients whom I interviewed supplemented their welfare checks without telling their Public Assistance caseworkers. The typical welfare mother in Chicago roughly doubled her cash income from AFDC in this way*" (1993, xiv–xv, emphasis added; see also Gardiner and Lyman, 1983).

13. In many of the interviews, one gets the sense that they almost fear touching the law by turning to legal services or requesting a fair hearing. When law is touched, caseworkers get angry, cases are inspected, things get

out of control, and thus, perhaps, they make the decision to simply stay away from what is, after all, a decidedly unpromising route (see Bumiller 1987; Sarat 1990, 362).

14. Joe Soss's recent research (1999) supports the efficacy of looking, as we do here, to the clients' relationships with agency practices and personnel. Trying to understand low levels of political engagement among AFDC clients, Soss in his study demonstrates that we should turn our attention to the ways that the welfare poor interact with and experience the agencies themselves. "To AFDC clients, silence in the face of consequential decision-making processes appears rational because they come to believe that speaking out is ineffective and risky." He concludes: "AFDC clients developed a characteristic set of beliefs about the agency and its power in relation to them. First, they came to see the agency as a pervasive threat in their life, as a potent force whose limits were unclear. Second, they perceived their welfare relationships as one-way transactions in which the agency had the authority to issue directives, and client status limited their options to either compliance or exit. Third, their view of agency decision making emphasized the personal discretion of individual workers rather than the rules of the institutions. Fourth, they came to understand the agency's capacity for action as an autonomous power over them, rather than as the power to act on their behalf" (1999, 366).

15. In *Power and Powerlessness* (1980), John Gaventa described and analyzed the multiple dimensions of powerlessness that pervaded the life of a small Appalachian community. In the most subtle dimension, widespread fatalism and ignorance prevented people from recognizing potential political and legal grievances. Were they to recognize these grievances, they faced another dimension of powerlessness in the inability to gain effective access to public forums and gain further mobilization around their issues. And if they were able to mobilize their issues, they were simply outgunned by the money, lawyers, and resources of the town's absentee mine owners. It is the same, if not even more overwhelming, sort of multidimensional powerlessness that we see here. See Gaventa's discussion of the widely noted quiescence of the Appalachian poor (1980, 33–44).

16. In *Unruly Practices*, Nancy Fraser argues that a gendering of social welfare systems in the United States divides systems between entitlement programs such as unemployment and social security, which deal with largely male citizens with "rights" to money, and welfare programs such as Food Stamps, AFDC, and Medicaid, which involve dependent and largely female clients. The former, male programs, involve less surveillance, less degradation, and less work on the part of beneficiaries:

> In sum, "masculine" social insurance schemes position recipients primarily as *rights-bearers*. The beneficiaries of these programs are not stigmatized. Neither administrative practice nor popular discourse constitutes them as "on the dole." They are constituted rather as receiving what they deserve ... what they have a *right* to. ...
>
> All this stands in stark contrast to the "feminine" sector of the U.S. social-welfare system. ... The relief programs are notorious

for the varieties of humiliation they inflict upon clients. They require considerable work in qualifying and maintaining eligibility, and they have a heavy component of surveillance. . . . Indeed, the only sense in which the category of rights is relevant to these clients' situation is the somewhat dubious one according to which they are entitled to treatment governed by the standard of formal bureaucratic rationality [and even that] is widely and routinely disregarded. (1989, 151, 152; see also Gordon 1994, 294–295)

17. "[P]eople who have experienced discriminatory treatment resist engagement in legal tactics because they stand in awe of the power of the law to disrupt their daily lives. At the same time, they are cynical about the power of the law actually to help them secure the jobs, housing, and other opportunities they lay claim to." (Bumiller 1988, 109)

18. Such a crisp distinction between "law's vocabulary" and other ways of speaking may overstate the extent to which different language claims can be categorized and understate the malleability and reach of legal discourse. See Waldron 1996.

Chapter Four

1. Historian Linda Gordan has observed that the design of the AFDC (Aid to Families with Dependent Children) program—the means test, the insufficient stipends—means that the frontline bureaucrats, the caseworkers, "knew that their clients had to supplement their incomes somehow" and that the "system turned workers once intended to be professional social workers into a bureaucratic police, for whom doing their jobs right encouraged clients' silence and cunning" (Gordon 1994, 297–298). There is no doubting that the design of AFDC helps to create a bureaucratic police force out of the caseworkers in the welfare agencies. Below, however, we meet some who resist this role.

2. See, for example, Ewick and Silbey 1992, 1998; Scott 1985, 1990; Yngvesson 1993; Sarat 1990; Merry 1990; White 1990; Genovese 1976.

3. "Resistance," as we mean it here, has been defined by James Scott as, "any act(s) by member(s) of a subordinate class that is or are *intended* either to mitigate or deny claims (for example, rents, taxes, prestige) made on that class by superordinate classes (for example, landlords, large farmers, the state) or to advance its own claims (for example, work, land, charity, respect) vis-à-vis those superordinate classes" (1985, 290).

4. In his 1992 presidential address to the Law and Society Association and his subsequent article entitled "Postmodernism, Protest, and the New Social Movements," Handler distinguishes between different generations of scholarly studies regarding "protests from below"—the struggles on the part of relatively powerless groups such as American slaves, welfare families, and impoverished individuals. Handler argues that a first generation of works—Genovese, Stack, Piven and Cloward—and a second, "postmodern" set of works—Silbey and Ewick, Sarat, Lucie White—share an interest in everyday resistance as a form of politics. But where the first generation centered on how the politics of everyday resistance lead to the building of bonds, soli-

darity, and new terms and languages that could, in turn, lead to new forms of empowerment and mobilization, the second generation, bent on deconstructionism and symbolic action, keeps its attention on individualistic acts of defiance and opposition with little attention to questions of solidarity, organized politics, material outcomes, and new opportunities (1992, 710–716). The analysis presented here has its footing in the second generation but attempts to respond to the important challenges raised in Handler's critique (see also McCann and March 1995).

5. As a local nurse in *The Unquiet Earth*, one of Denise Giardina's novels of Appalachian life, put it, "I decided it is better for a person to steal what they need than to be given it, because when they steal they are at least doing it for themselves" (1992, 68).

6. In responding to such critique, Ewick and Silbey (1998) argue that "[t]o dismiss everyday forms of resistance on the grounds that they are individualistic, unprincipled, and temporary is to foreclose crucial questions about the relationship between power and resistance. Although resistance may be opportunistic and individualistic, it is neither random nor idiosyncratic. The opportunities for resistance emerge from the regular exercise of power. . . . Through everyday practical engagements, individuals identify the cracks and vulnerabilities of organized power and institutions such as the law" (187).

7. People must also live in fear of each other, since the "rat call" is still a very important means through which the state discovers rule-breakers.

8. "It is no coincidence that the cries of 'bread,' 'land,' and 'no taxes' that so often lie at the core of peasant rebellion are all joined to the basic material survival needs of the peasant household. Nor should it be anything more than a commonplace that everyday peasant politics and everyday peasant resistance (and also, of course, everyday peasant compliance) flows from these same fundamental material needs." (Scott 1985, 295)

9. The tension between the two ethics or perspectives is succinctly stated in this excerpt from *Women and Moral Theory*, edited by Eva Kittay and Diana Meyers: "The morality of rights and formal reasoning is the one familiar to us from the liberal tradition of Locke, Kant, and, most recently, Rawls. It posits an autonomous moral agent who discovers and applies a set of fundamental rules through the use of universal and abstract reason. The morality of care and responsibility is an alternate set of moral concerns that Gilligan believes she has encountered in her investigation of women's moral decision-making. Here the central preoccupation is a responsiveness to others that dictates providing care, preventing harm, and maintaining relationships" (1987, 3; see also Gilligan 1982, 20; and White 2000, chap. 3).

10. Linda Gordon's history of women and welfare prior to the New Deal notes the importance of maternalist arguments and observes that advocates for welfare would use rights claims, needs claims, and compensation-for-services arguments in "complementary, not alternative" manners, and that "men more often made rights claims" (1994, 160).

11. McCann's research identified some roughly parallel debates in the comparable worth movement (1994, 236–237).

12. Edin and Lein (1997) have found that some fathers, publicly vilified as "deadbeat dads" due to their failure to pay child support, actually do pro-

vide significant support to their children but keep it off the books to avoid reducing the children's benefits from public assistance programs (160–161).

CHAPTER FIVE

1. Gavison (1980) has an eleven-page discussion on why privacy is important to the individual and a single page on privacy in a social context.

2. There are, obviously, risks to be taken and calculations to be made. In the 1980s, for example, it probably seemed wiser to battle employee drug testing with a privacy right, than with a debate over the use of marijuana (the primary substance detected in drug-testing programs). But clearly, the former strategy was not all that successful, and perhaps a turn to the latter would have engaged more people in a more widespread conversation about social policy.

REFERENCES

Abramowitz, Mimi. 1988. *Regulating the Lives of Women: Social Welfare Policy from Colonial Times to the Present*. Boston: South End Press.

Agre, Philip E., and Marc Rotenberg, eds. 1997. *Technology and Privacy: The New Landscape*. Cambridge: MIT Press.

Allen, Anita L. 1988. *Uneasy Access: Privacy for Women in a Free Society*. Totowa, N.J.: Rowman and Littlefield.

Bachrach, Peter, and Morton S. Baratz. 1962. "The Two Faces of Power." *American Political Science Review* 56, no. 4:947–952.

Bell, Winifred. 1965. *Aid to Dependent Children*. New York: Columbia University Press.

Bennett, Colin J., and Rebecca Grant, eds. 1999. *Visions of Privacy: Policy Choices for the Digital Age*. Toronto: University of Toronto Press.

Brodkin, Evelyn, and Michael Lipsky. 1983. "Quality Control in AFDC as an Administrative Strategy." *Social Service Review* March: 1–34.

Bumiller, Kristin. 1987. "Victims in the Shadow of the Law: A Critique of the Model of Legal Protection." *Signs* 12:421–439.

———. 1988. *The Civil Rights Society: The Social Construction of Victims*. Baltimore: Johns Hopkins University Press.

Bussiere, Elizabeth. 1997. *(Dis)Entitling the Poor: The Warren Court, Welfare Rights, and the American Political Tradition*. University Park: Pennsylvania State University Press.

Caudill, Harry M. 1963. *Night Comes to the Cumberlands: A Biography of a Depressed Area*. Boston: Little, Brown.

Congressional Research Service. 1977. *Administration of the AFDC Program*. Washington, D.C.: Government Printing Office.

Copelon, Rhonda. 1989. "Beyond the Liberal Idea of Privacy: Toward a Right of Autonomy." In *Judging the Constitution*, edited by Michael McCann and Gerald Houseman, pp. 287–314. Boston: Scott Foresman.

Dandeker, Christopher. 1990. *Surveillance, Power, and Modernity: Bureaucracy and Discipline from 1700 to the Present Day*. New York: St. Martin's.

Davies, Simon. 1997. "Re-engineering the Right to Privacy: How Privacy Has Been Transformed from a Right to a Commodity." In *Technology and Privacy: The New Landscape*, edited by Philip E. Agre and Marc Rotenberg, pp. 143–165. Cambridge: MIT Press.

————. 1999. "Spanners in the Works: How the Privacy Movement Is Adapting to the Challenge of Big Brother." In *Visions of Privacy: Policy Choices for the Digital Age*, edited by Colin J. Bennett and Rebecca Grant, 244–262. Toronto: University of Toronto Press.

Davis, Martha F. 1993. *Brutal Need: Lawyers and the Welfare Rights Movement, 1960–1973.* New Haven: Yale University Press.

Dery, David. 1981. *Computers in Welfare: The MIS-Match.* Beverly Hills: Sage.

Edelman, Murray. 1988. *Constructing the Political Spectacle.* Chicago: University of Chicago Press.

Edin, Kathryn. 1993. *There's a Lot of Month Left at the End of the Money: How Welfare Recipients Make Ends Meet in Chicago.* New York: Garland.

Edin, Kathryn, and Laura Lein. 1997. *Making Ends Meet: How Single Mothers Survive Welfare and Low-Wage Work.* New York: Russell Sage Foundation.

Engel, David M. 1984. "The Oven Bird's Song: Insiders, Outsiders, and Personal Injuries in an American Community." *Law and Society Review* 18, no. 4:551–582.

Engel, David M., and Frank W. Munger. 1996. "Rights, Remembrance, and the Reconciliation of Difference." *Law and Society Review* 30, no. 1:7–54.

Epp, Charles R. 1998. *The Rights Revolution: Lawyers, Activists, and Supreme Courts in Comparative Perspective.* Chicago: University of Chicago Press.

Ewick, Patricia. 1992. "Postmodern Melancholia," *Law and Society Review* 26, no. 4:755–764.

Ewick, Patricia, and Susan S. Silbey. 1992. "Conformity, Contestation, and Resistance: An Account of Legal Consciousness." *New England Law Review* 26:731–749.

————. 1998. *The Common Place of Law.* Chicago: University of Chicago Press.

Ferguson, Kathy E. 1984. *The Feminist Case against Bureaucracy.* Philadelphia: Temple University Press.

Flaherty, David. 1989. *Protecting Privacy in Surveillance Societies.* Chapel Hill: University of North Carolina Press.

————. 1997. "Controlling Surveillance: Can Privacy Protection Be Made Effective?" In *Technology and Privacy: The New Landscape*, edited by Philip E. Agre and Marc Rotenberg, pp. 167–192. Cambridge: MIT Press.

Foucault, Michel. 1979. *Discipline and Punish.* New York: Vintage.

————. 1980. *Power/Knowledge*, edited by Colin Gordon. New York: Pantheon.

Fraser, Nancy. 1989. *Unruly Practices: Power, Discourse, and Gender in Contemporary Social Theory.* Minneapolis: University of Minnesota Press.

————. 1990. "Struggle over Needs: Outline of a Socialist-Feminist Critical Theory of Late-Capitalist Political Culture." In *Women, the State, and Welfare*, edited by Linda Gordon, pp. 199–225. Madison: University of Wisconsin Press.

Gandy, Oscar H. 1993. *The Panoptic Sort: A Political Economy of Personal Information*. Boulder: Westview Press.

Gardiner, John A., and Theodore R. Lyman. 1983. *Responses to Fraud and Abuse in AFDC and Medicaid Programs*. Washington, D.C.: National Institute of Justice.

————. 1984. *The Fraud Control Game: State Responses to Fraud and Abuse in AFDC and Medicaid Programs*. Bloomington: Indiana University Press.

Gaventa, John. 1980. *Power and Powerlessness: Quiescence and Rebellion in an Appalachian Valley*. Urbana: University of Illinois Press.

Gavison, Ruth. 1980. "Privacy and the Limits of Law." *Yale Law Journal* 89, no. 3:421–471.

Gellman, Robert. 1997. "Does Privacy Law Work?" In *Technology and Privacy: The New Landscape*, edited by Philip E. Agre and Marc Rotenberg, pp. 193–218. Cambridge: MIT Press.

Genovese, Eugene D. 1976. *Roll, Jordan, Roll*. New York: Pantheon.

Giardina, Denise. 1992. *The Unquiet Earth*. New York: Norton.

Gilligan, Carol. 1982. *In a Different Voice: Psychological Theory and Women's Development*. Cambridge: Harvard University Press.

Gilliom, John. 1994. *Surveillance, Privacy, and the Law: Employee Drug Testing and the Politics of Social Control*. Ann Arbor: University of Michigan Press.

————. 1997. "Everyday Surveillance, Everyday Resistance: Computer Monitoring in the Lives of the Appalachian Poor." *Studies in Law, Politics, and Society* 16, edited by Austin Sarat and Susan Silbey, pp. 275–297. Greenwich, Conn.: JAI Press.

Glendon, Mary Ann. 1991. *Rights Talk: The Impoverishment of Political Discourse*. New York: Free Press.

Gordon, Linda. 1994. *Pitied But Not Entitled: Single Mothers and the History of Welfare 1890–1935*. New York: Free Press.

Gordon, Linda, ed. 1990. *Women, the State, and Welfare*. Madison: University of Wisconsin Press.

Greenberg, David, and Douglas Wolf, with Jennifer Pfiester. 1986. *Using Computers to Combat Welfare Fraud*. Westport, Conn.: Greenwood Press.

Halperin, Rhoda. 1990. *The Livelihood of Kin: Making Ends Meet "The Kentucky Way."* Austin: University of Texas Press.

Handler, Joel F. 1973. *The Coercive Social Worker: British Lessons for American Social Services*. Madison: University of Wisconsin Insitute for Research on Poverty.

————. 1978. *Social Movements and the Legal System: A Theory of Law Reform and Social Change*. New York: Academic Press.

———. 1979. *Protecting the Social Service Client.* New York: Academic Press.

———. 1992. "Postmodernism, Protest, and the New Social Movements." *Law and Society Review* 26, no. 4:697–732.

Handler, Joel F., and Yeheskel Hasenfeld. 1991. *The Moral Construction of Poverty: Welfare Reform in America.* Newbury Park, Cal.: Sage Publications.

Handler, Joel F., and Margaret K. Rosenheim. 1966. "Privacy in Welfare: Public Assistance and Juvenile Justice." *Law and Contemporary Problems* 31:377–412.

Harris, Beth. 1999. "Representing Homeless Families: Repeat Player Implementation Strategies." *Law and Society Review* 33, no. 4:911–940.

Hertz, Susan Handley. 1981. *The Welfare Mothers Movement: A Decade of Change for Poor Women?* Washington, D.C.: University Press of America.

Hunt, Alan. 1985. "The Ideology of Law: Advances and Problems in Recent Applications of the Concept of Ideology to the Analysis of Law." *Law and Society Review* 19, no. 1:1–37.

Katz, Michael B. 1986. *In the Shadow of the Poorhouse: A Social History of Welfare in America.* New York: Basic Books.

Kiss, Elizabeth. 1997. "Alchemy or Fool's Gold? Assessing Feminist Doubts about Rights." In *Reconstructing Political Theory: Feminist Perspectives,* edited by Mary Lyndon Shanley and Uma Narayan, pp. 1–24. University Park: Pennsylvania State University Press.

Kittay, Eva Feder, and Diana T. Meyers, eds. 1987. *Women and Moral Theory.* Savage, Md.: Roman and Littlefield.

Kuhn, Thomas. 1962. *The Structure of Scientific Revolutions.* Chicago: University of Chicago Press.

Koven, Seth, and Sonya Michel, eds., 1993. *Mothers of a New World: Maternalist Politics and the Origins of Welfare States.* New York: Routledge.

Ladd-Taylor, Molly. 1994. *Mother-Work: Women, Child Welfare, and the State, 1890–1930.* Urbana: University of Illinois Press.

Lester, Toby. 2001. "The Reinvention of Privacy." *Atlantic Monthly* 287, no. 3 (March): 27–39.

MacKinnon, Catherine A. 1993. "Reflections on Law in the Everyday Life of Women." In *Law in Everyday Life,* edited by Austin Sarat and Thomas Kearns, pp. 109–122. Ann Arbor: University of Michigan Press.

Marx, Gary. 1986. "The Iron Fist in the Velvet Glove: Totalitarian Potentials Within Democratic Structures." In *The Social Fabric: Dimensions and Issues,* edited by James Short. Beverly Hills, Cal.: Sage.

———. 1999. "Ethics for the New Surveillance." In *Visions of Privacy: Policy Choices for the Digital Age,* edited by Colin J. Bennett and Rebecca Grant, pp. 39–67. Toronto: University of Toronto Press.

Marx, Gary, and Nancy Reichman. 1984. "Routinizing the Discovery of Secrets." *American Behavioral Scientist* 27, no. 4:423–452.

McCann, Michael. 1994. *Rights at Work: Pay Equity Reform and the Politics of Legal Mobilization.* Chicago: University of Chicago Press.

McCann, Michael, and Tracey March. 1995. "Law and Everyday Forms of Resistance." In *Studies in Law, Politics, and Society* 15, edited by Austin Sarat and Susan Silbey, pp. 201–236. Greenwich, Conn.: JAI Press.

Merry, Sally Engle. 1990. *Getting Justice and Getting Even: Legal Consciousness among Working Class Americans.* Chicago: University of Chicago Press.

———. 1995. "Resistance and the Cultural Power of Law." *Law and Society Review* 29, no. 1:11–26.

Meyers, Diana T., and Eva Feder Kittay. 1987. Introduction to *Women and Moral Theory*, edited by Eva Feder Kittay and Diana T. Meyers. Savage, Md.: Roman and Littlefield.

Milner, Neal. 1989. "The Denigration of Rights and the Persistance of Rights Talk: A Cultural Portrait." *Law and Social Inquiry* 14:631–675.

Minow, Martha. 1990. *Making All the Difference: Inclusion, Exclusion, and American Law.* Ithaca, N.Y.: Cornell University Press.

Nock, Steven L. 1993. *The Costs of Privacy: Surveillance and Reputation in America.* New York: A. De Gruyter.

Piven, Frances Fox, and Richard A. Cloward. 1972. *Regulating the Poor: The Functions of Public Welfare.* New York: Vintage Books.

———. 1979. *Poor People's Movements: Why They Succeed, How They Fail.* New York: Vintage Books.

Polakow, Valerie. 1992. *Lives on the Edge: Single Mothers and Their Children in the Other America.* Chicago: University of Chicago Press.

Regan, Priscilla M. 1995. *Legislating Privacy: Technology, Social Values, and Public Policy.* Chapel Hill: University of North Carolina Press.

Reich, Charles. 1963. "Midnight Searches and the Social Security Act." *Yale Law Journal* 72:1347–1360.

———. 1965. "Individual Rights and Social Welfare: Emerging Legal Issues." *Yale Law Journal* 74:1245–1257.

Reichman, Nancy. 1987. "Computer Matching: Toward Computerized Systems of Regulation." *Law and Policy* October: 387–415.

Rose, Nikolas. 1999. *Powers of Freedom: Reframing Political Thought.* Cambridge: Cambridge University Press.

Rosen, Jeffrey. 2000. "The Eroded Self." *New York Times Magazine,* April 30.

Rosenberg, Gerald N. 1991. *The Hollow Hope: Can Courts Bring About Social Change?* Chicago: University of Chicago Press.

Rule, James B. 1973. *Private Lives and Public Surveillance.* London: Allen Lane.

Rule, James, Douglas McCadam, Linda Stearns, and David Uglow. 1980. *The Politics of Privacy.* New York: Elsevier.

Sarat, Austin. 1990. "The Law Is All Over: Power, Resistance, and the Legal Consciousness of the Welfare Poor." *Yale Journal of Law and the Humanities* 2:343–379.

Sarat, Austin, and Thomas Kearns. 1993. "Beyond the Great Divide: Forms of Legal Scholarship and Everyday Life." In *Law in Everyday Life*, edited by Austin Sarat and Thomas Kearns, pp. 21–61. Ann Arbor: University of Michigan Press.

Scheingold, Stuart. 1974. *The Politics of Rights: Lawyers, Public Policy, and Political Change.* New Haven: Yale University Press.

———. 1989. "Constitutional Rights and Social Change." In *Judging the Constitution*, edited by Michael McCann and Gerald Houseman, pp. 73–91. Boston: Scott Foresman.

Schneider, Elizabeth M. 1986. "The Dialectic of Rights and Politics: Perspectives from the Women's Movement." *New York University Law Review* 61:589–652.

Scott, James C. 1985. *Weapons of the Weak: Everyday Forms of Peasant Resistance.* New Haven: Yale University Press.

———. 1990. *Domination and the Arts of Resistance: Hidden Transcripts.* New Haven: Yale University Press.

———. 1998. *Seeing like a State: How Certain Schemes to Improve the Human Condition Have Failed.* New Haven: Yale University Press.

Seipp, David J. 1978. *The Right to Privacy in American History.* Cambridge: Harvard University Program on Information Resources Policy.

Sevenhuijsen, Selma. 1998. *Citizenship and the Ethics of Care: Feminist Considerations on Justice, Morality, and Politics*, trans. by Liz Savage. New York: Routledge.

Shanley, Mary Lyndon, and Uma Narayan, eds. 1997. *Reconstructing Political Theory: Feminist Perspectives.* University Park: Pennsylvania State University Press.

Silbey, Susan, and Austin Sarat. 1987. "Critical Traditions in Law and Society Research." *Law and Society Review* 21, no. 1:165–174.

Silverstein, Helena. 1996. *Unleashing Rights.* Ann Arbor: University of Michigan Press.

Skocpol, Theda. 1992. *Protecting Soldiers and Mothers: The Political Origins of Social Policy in the United States.* Cambridge: Harvard University Press.

Smith, Rogers M. 1988. "Political Jurisprudence, The 'New Institutionalism,' and the Future of Public Law." *American Political Science Review* 82, no. 1:89–108.

Soss, Joe. 1999. "Lessons of Welfare: Policy Design, Political Learning, and Political Action." *American Political Science Review* 93, no. 2:363–380.

Stack, Carol B. 1974. *All Our Kin: Strategies for Survival in a Black Community.* New York: Harper and Row.

Tagg, John. 1988. *The Burden of Representation: Essays on Photographies and Histories.* Amherst: University of Massachusetts Press.

Thompson, E. P. 1975. *Whigs and Hunters: The Origins of the Black Act.* New York: Pantheon.

Tocqueville, Alexis de. 1969 [orig. publ. 1835-40]. *Democracy in America*, edited by J. P. Mayer. New York: Anchor Books.

Torpey, John. 2000. *The Invention of the Passport: Surveillance, Citizenship, and the State.* Cambridge: Cambridge University Press.

Trattner, Walter I. 1999. *From Poor Law to Welfare State: A History of Social Welfare in America.* New York: Free Press.

Tronto, Joan C. 1993. *Moral Boundaries: A Political Argument for an Ethic of Care.* London: Routledge.

Tushnet, Mark. 1984. "An Essay on Rights." *Texas Law Review* 62:1363–1403.

Verba, Sidney, Kay Lehman Schlozman, and Henry E. Brady. 1995. *Voice and Equality: Civic Voluntarism in American Politics.* Cambridge: Harvard University Press.

Waldron, Jeremy. 1996. "Rights and Needs: The Myth of Disjunction." In *Legal Rights: Historical and Philosophical Perspectives,* edited by Austin Sarat and Thomas Kearns. Ann Arbor: University of Michigan Press.

Warren, Samuel D., and Louis D. Brandeis. 1890. "The Right to Privacy." *Harvard Law Review* 4:193–220.

Westin, Alan F. 1967. *Privacy and Freedom.* New York: Atheneum.

Westwood, John. 1999. "Life in the Privacy Trenches: Experiences of the British Columbia Civil Liberties Association." In *Visions of Privacy: Policy Choices for the Digital Age,* edited by Colin J. Bennett and Rebecca Grant, pp. 231–243. Toronto: University of Toronto Press.

Whitaker, Reg. 1999. *The End of Privacy: How Total Surveillance Is Becoming a Reality.* New York: New Press.

White, Julie Anne. 2000. *Democracy, Justice, and the Welfare State: Reconstructing Public Care.* University Park: Pennsylvania State University Press.

White, Lucie. 1990. "Subordination, Rhetorical Survival Skills, and Sunday Shoes: Notes on the Hearing of Mrs. G." *Buffalo Law Review* 38:1–58.

Williams, Patricia. 1987. "Alchemical Notes: Reconstructing Ideals from Deconstructed Rights." *Harvard Civil Rights–Civil Liberties Law Review* 22:410–433.

Yngvesson, Barbara. 1993. *Virtuous Citizens, Disruptive Subjects: Order and Complaint in a New England Court.* New York: Routledge.

Zemans, Frances. 1983. "Legal Mobilization: The Neglected Role of the Law in the Political System." *American Political Science Review* 77, no. 3:690–703.

Zuboff, Shoshana. 1988. *In the Age of the Smart Machine: The Future of Work and Power.* New York: Basic Books.

INDEX

abandonment, "right" of, 122–23
Abenaki Indian Tribe, 115–17
able-bodied poor: defining, 22; strategies against, 23–24, 39, 155n.2
ACLU (American Civil Liberties Union), 10, 141, 147
affirmative action, 83. *See also* pay equity movement
African Americans, 10, 27, 29, 112
Agre, Philip E., 2, 153n.1
Aid to Families with Dependent Children (AFDC): bureaucratic policing of, 163n.1; child support and, 31–32, 72; clients' beliefs about, 162n.14; computer matching by, 115, 116; declaration era and, 28–29, 38, 156n.8; eligibility rules for, 26–27, 155nn. 4, 6; entitlement programs vs., 27–28, 127–28; establishment of, 26; fraud and error in, 156n.8; "getting around" rules of, 48–49; income provided from, 43–44, 67, 69, 87–88, 161n.12; precursors to, 25; QC movement and, 30; state administration of, 33, 158n.1; transience in, 66, 160n.12. *See also* welfare programs
alcohol testing, 127
alerts, IEVS match, 36–37, 157n.14
Allen, Anita L., 121
almsgiving laws, 21–22
almshouse era, 23–24
ambivalence, welfare abuse and, 61–63
American Civil Liberties Union (ACLU), 10, 141, 147
Amy (interviewee), on resistance, 95
anger, rights violations and, xi, 140–44
antisurveillance activism, 102

antisurveillance "politics." *See* everyday resistance; resistance
Appalachian Ohio: declaration era in, 29; poverty in, 43, 44, 89; power of surveillance in, 4–5, 132–33
Appalachian poor: diversity among, 65–66; everyday resistance by, 103–6, 112–14, 164n.5; generalizing findings about, 118–19; powerlessness of, 44, 90–91, 92, 162n.15; similarities among, 66. *See also* "poor," the; welfare poor
application process: client rights and, 80–82; complaints about, 74–75, 76–77; CRIS-E and, 34–35, 156n.12; describing, 48, 52–53, 56, 58–60, 61–62; examples of, 17–18. *See also* eligibility determination
Athens County Department of Human Services, 34–35
attorneys. *See* lawyers
authoritarian surveillance, 41–42
authority, institutional, 84, 161n.10
automobiles, relief eligibility and, 17–18, 19
autonomy, individual: caseworkers' struggle for, 97; illusions of, 148; loss of, 6–7, 129, 150; maintaining zone of, 104–5; "rights" of, 122–23

Baker, Cindy (interviewer), xiv; Delilah and, 94; Dewey and, 93; Eliza and, 58–61; Elizabeth and, 95; Jamaica and, 74–75; Jessica and, 80–82; Marilyn and, 61–64; Moonstar and, 78; Sally and, 56–57
bank accounts, unreported, 53, 55

control, external. *See* domination
control, personal: asserting, 6–7, 20; legal battle over, 115–17; loss of, 129, 150
cooperation, welfare clients and, 106–7
Copelon, Rhonda, 121
Cover, Robert, 72
creative force, power as, 130–31
Criminal Identification and Investigation, Ohio State Bureau of, 138
CRIS-E: benefits of, 157n.13; clients' knowledge of, 50, 57, 63–64; complaints about, 73–78, 98; description of, 1, 4–5, 33–37, 156n.12; feelings about, 54–55, 57, 66–67. *See also* Client Information Systems; surveillance programs; welfare surveillance

Dandeker, Christopher, 2, 21, 27, 35
Dandridge v. Williams, 72–73
"data protection" model, 153n.1
Davies, Simon, 4, 102, 124, 154n.6
Davis, Billy G., 158n.16
Davis, Martha F., 10, 71, 111, 160n.3
"deadbeat dads," 31, 164n.12
declaration era, 28–29, 38, 73, 156nn. 7, 8
Deficit Reduction Act (1984), 156n.11
Delilah (interviewee), on resistance, 94, 109
Dempsey, John, 32
Department of Human Services (Ohio): antifraud campaigns of, 89; assistance from, 89–90; Athens County, 34–35; food stamp coaching by, 97–98; "rat calls" to, 36, 87; resistance to, 95–96; statements by, 18, 155n.1
dependency: feelings about, 51, 77, 78; privacy rights and, 124; struggles against, 104, 164n.5
depression-era relief, 17–18, 19, 25–26
Dery, David, 157n.13
deterrence policies: emphasis on, 13–14, 27, 28; strategies of, 23–24, 39
Dewey (interviewee), on resistance, 93
Discipline and Punish (Foucault), 107, 130–31, 132, 133
discrimination, legal consciousness and, 163n.17
disempowerment. *See* powerlessness
(Dis)Entitling the Poor (Bussiere), 110
DNA testing, 31, 32, 134
domination: panopticon and, 130–31;

resistance to, 51–52, 95–96; shifts in, 128–29; struggles over, 105; surveillance politics and, 2–3, 9, 16; traditional form of, 129–30
"driver," CRIS-E's, 34–35, 156n.12
drug-testing programs, 101–2, 127, 165n.2
drugs, "war" on, 127, 139–40
due process, debate over, 4, 5, 70

Edin, Kathryn, 43; on "deadbeat dads," 164n.12; "snowball" sampling by, 46; on welfare budgets, 48, 87, 88, 95, 104, 161n.12
elderly, social welfare for, 25–26, 127–28, 155n.4
Eleanor (interviewee), on fear, 87
eligibility determination: client obligations for, 155n.6; complexity of, 157n.13; CRIS-E and, 34, 156n.12; declaration method for, 28–29; deterrence through, 23–24, 39; disparities in, 27–28, 127–28; "means test" for, 13, 20, 27; policies for, 17–18, 19, 25–26, 27, 155n.4; recertification and, 50–51; residency requirements and, 72. *See also* application process
Eliza (interviewee), on struggle, 58–61, 65
Elizabeth (interviewee), on resistance, 95
employee drug testing, 101–2, 127, 165n.2
employment, 89
empowerment: information and, 86–87, 148; law and, 80–83; rights approach to, 90–91, 92. *See also* power
Engel, David M., 11, 83, 153n.3, 154n.5
entitlement programs: creation of, 25–26; obtaining data on, 35–37, 158n.16; welfare vs., 27–28, 127–28, 155n.4, 162n.16
epistemology: of "the poor," 37–40; in research, 67, 160n.13. *See also* knowledge systems
Epp, Charles R., 10
equality, political, conflict over, 110
errors, administrative: CRIS-E and, 157n.12; declaration era and, 156n.8; eliminating, 116
ethics: of care, 6, 15, 109–12, 164n.9; of rights, 123; surveillance and, 77
everyday resistance: assessing, 103–6; benefits of, 6–7, 15–16, 112–13;